MONEY Keep what you earn!

MONEY KEEP WHAT YOU EARN!

AND SAVE YOURSELF A FINANCIAL PLAN

Stop giving your money to credit cards, mortgage banks, car dealers, Wall Street crooks, and tax collectors!

Wealth is a choice poverty is the result of not making that choice. Choose wealth!

DAVID DORSEY CPA
Basic Course

QUOTES TO CONSIDER:
"I have had a little money and I have had a lot of money, having a lot of money is better"

"A man with money can control the circumstances of his life; a man without money is controlled by them"

"I have travel the world over, read hundreds of books and I have never found one downside to having money"

"I've heard that money is the root of evil…this is not true, _not_ having money is the root of evil"

This book is dedicated to anyone who wants to be able to control the circumstances of life.

This manual designed to provide accurate and authoritative information about the subject matter discussed. It is sold with the understanding that the publisher and the author are not engaged in rendering legal or accounting service or advice. If legal, accounting, or other expert assistance is required, the services of a competent professional should be sought.

ISBN: 1516889789
ISBN 13: 9781516889785

To my mother:
Minerva Dorsey
Thank you for giving me life, twice.

CONTENTS

INTRODUCTION

DUPED-THE AMERICAN DREAM LIE

H AVE YOU EVER wondered how in the richest country on earth, that you can work your entire life, earn a million dollars or more, and end up flat broke with nothing, depending upon the government for your survival and a failed healthcare system? That's because we all have been duped by the system into the American dream lie. You see we all have been taught by big business and the government's school system on how to earn money: *Just do what they say and get a job.* However, have you ever wondered why these same people never teaches us how to keep what we earn so we can be the beneficiary of a lifetime of labor? It's because they benefit from us being a consumer and spending all that we earn. We must save ourselves because no one is looking out for us. Not the taxing government, big business nor the banks.

In America today, millions upon millions of Americans are fighting, protesting, and calling on the politicians to give them a minimum wage. Can you believe that? They are fighting for a minimum wage. They should be fighting for a maximum wage not a minimum! A couple of extra dollars an hour only leads to a long-term consumer poverty lifestyle. This course is not about chasing or becoming wealthy. It's about realizing that you are already wealthy, but you make yourself poor with a consumer mentality. How to keep what you earn is a mindset. It's the mindset that one realizes that no one is coming to save you from poverty. You see I have learned that wealth is a choice and poverty is a result from not making that choice. You must learn how to keep the money that you earn, use it to make you wealthy and free. Why choose wealth you say? Because you can't depend on nor can you trust the politicians for your survival. Wealth and money buys what you really want, freedom from the system, a boss, and a job! To free yourself you must stop giving your money to credit cards, mortgage banks, big business, wall street crooks and tax collectors. Learn to use your money to make yourself wealthy.

DIY! And what is wealth? Wealth is no more than the ability to live comfortably off the income from your own personal resources. Whether that's $1,000 a month or a $1,000,000, it's all the same. It's all about investing your saving in things that produces income for life. And this is easier than you think.

You see we are all living a lie! If you are like most of us, the system has duped you. Who is the system you asked? The system is the taxing governments, politicians, mortgage banks, and big business. They created the American dream lie and it doesn't work. Why? Because, the dream that they sold us, benefits the system not us! This dream lie literally sucks the money out of your pocket into theirs. So, what is the American dream lie? Well, you heard it before; you go to school make good grades so you can get a good job with benefits. You get married have 2 and ¼ children. You buy a big house with a 30-year mortgage so you can afford the monthly payments. Then you squirrel a little money away for your retirement so you can live out your golden years traveling the world. Sound good huh? Well it's all a lie and here are the facts to prove it compiled by researcher's PRWEB.

1. According to a study by US Dept. of Health & Human Services, 96% of Americans never achieve financial independence. They end up depending on charity, welfare, family, or are forced to keep working past their retirement age.

2. According to the IRS, 85% of the people reaching age 65 years don't have even $200 in their bank accounts!

3. US Census Bureau says that 97% of Americans never realize their dreams and desires in life, and are forced to retire on annual income of $10,000 or less!

4. Every day, about 2,200 Americans lose their jobs, while more than 20,000 families lose their homes to foreclosure every year and another 500,000 file for personal bankruptcy.

5. Some of the largest US corporations have been continuously downsizing their work force and laying off thousands of people during the past ten years.

6. America is weakening and sinking deeper into a debt nation.

7. The paradox is that America is the richest and greatest nation on earth and yet millions of the people live below the poverty level.

8. Why is it that 1% of the Americans control 37% of all wealth, 60% of all the corporations and 10% of all the real estate? One of the reasons is that most people do not know the secrets of the rich and powerful and are ignorant of the dynamics of wealth creation, preservation, and perpetuation.

9. The majority of the people have been misled to believe that to achieve financial security, success and happiness, all they have to do is to go to college, obtain a degree and get a job. Nothing can be further from the Truth!

Those are the facts folks. It looks like the system has declared a financial war on us. I mean they sold us on their system that take money out of our pockets and put it in theirs and we are left with nothing. That's why I feel such a strong urgency to tell you about this lie because it will not and have not brought you financial security or independence, which is the real American dream. When I say independence, I mean that you should not be dependent on anyone, not your parents, the government, your job, or grandma for that matter. I call it a state of un-vulnerability, meaning that you own your life. You keep what you earn and you use your money to make you wealthy not them. In that way, if something happens to you or you lose your job they can't come and take your life away from you.

In this course, you will learn a 3-step-by-step system that will guide you to:

1. **CUT THE EASY CREDIT OFF**

2. **CUT YOUR TAXES IN HALF**

3. **INVEST IN THINGS THAT PAY YOU INCOME FOR LIFE**

Rinse and repeat steps 1, 2 and 3 until wealthy. Let's get started.

Rule # 1:
Stop Thinking and Acting Like the Poor

THE FINANCIAL HABITS OF THE POOR

THE WORST FINANCIAL habit of the poor is that they spend more money than they earn. The only way to spend what you don't have is to get into debt. The weapon of choice that leads to your demise is credit cards. It doesn't matter who you are. It doesn't matter your race, gender, religion, social status, height, or weight. If you spend more than you earn you don't have a chance at financial security, and you can never be free. You will eventually belong to a class of people called the poor. It doesn't matter how much you earn whether its $1,000 a month or a $1,000,000 a month if you spend more than you earn you will always be poor. The financial habits of the poor are to be a consumer they spend first then save what's left. And usually there is nothing left to save. The poor live to consume and thinks in terms of paying for their purchases with debt. Their only concern is earning just enough money to make minimum payments. They live paycheck to paycheck and have no savings. Yes, just like the rest of us they will earn a million dollars or more over their working lives but will end up with none of it. They will have a house full of worthless depreciating things that has no value. The consumer runs their lives on autopilot meaning they do what everybody around them are doing. And everybody around them are broke. The consumer lives to consume not produce nor invest, this is the root cause of generational poverty.

So, we are followers following followers. But have you noticed that most people don't have any real wealth or financial security? Meaning that if they lose their jobs they lose everything. Seniors are downsizing from a 3-bedroom home to a small apartment that they can afford on their meager social security checks. They realize that they don't own anything, that their lifestyles were just loaned to them for as long as they could afford to make the minimum payments. Consumers are all one paycheck away from that other income bracket called, poor. If you drive down these neighborhoods around 10 am in the morning, you don't see anybody. Why? Because everybody is going to work to make minimum payments on the pile of debt that they owe to keep this life style of consumerism going. And this is where they spend their lives at work.

If you want to ever get out of this rat race, then you must immediately stop acting like a consumer. You must from this day forward began to adopt the mindset of the producer investor. If you have been working all your life and don't have any accumulated wealth the kind that will pay you income instead of you having to work for money, then you probably have been living the lifestyle of a consumer. We need to consume less and develop a Spending Plan that will put controls on our consumption. We need to consume less and invest more in income producing assets.

FINANCIAL *INSECURITY* THE NORM

*"If you don't find a way to make money
while you sleep, you will work until you die."*
Warren Buffett

A full 76% of Americans are living paycheck-to-paycheck and cannot afford to stop working. Never stop working! Most Americans are not familiar with the process to create wealth and financial security. Why else would you work for 40 to 50 years, earn on average a million dollars, and end up with none of it? It's because the system teaches us to be consumers not investors. Most of us have little to no emergency savings. Fewer than one in four Americans have enough money in their savings account to cover at least six months of expenses, enough to help cushion the blow of a job loss, medical emergency, or some other unexpected event, according to a survey of 1,000 adults. Meanwhile, 50% of those surveyed have less than a three-month cushion and 27% had no savings at all according to a CNN source.

Do you know the difference between an old man and an elderly gentleman? Money, income. I am asking you to choose wealth, not poverty. Keep in mind that you will work 40 to 50 years of your young adult life and your employers will not give you a pension to retire with dignity! When you lose your job, or stop working the money stops and you get no pension, you have no income. You will be lucky to work for the same employer until you retire. If you don't work for the same employer until you are 65 years old, then don't expect a pension. This is the main reason you must become financially secured before it's too late. Yes, I believe that you can count on Social Security, but this is a poverty retirement plan. It will not be enough to meet your basic living expenses. All you get is all you save. That's it! Financial insecurity seems to be the norm for most Americans. If we are honest with ourselves most of us are no more prepared for our financial futures than the day we left home. That's because we were sold this American dream lie, which is to be a consumer not an investor or a producer.

THE ILLUSION OF WEALTH

Most working Americans are under the illusion that just because we work and earn money this gives us a false sense of security and a feeling that we are wealthy. So, since we feel secured and wealthy we go out and buy everything that we can to match our feelings and this puts us on the fast track to poverty. Working for money is just an illusion of wealth, a dream. You will awaken from this dream if for whatever reason you lose that job and your income stops immediately. Have you ever lost a job that you or your family depended on the income for your survival? This is the feeling of poverty. This is what is waiting for you in your later years if you don't choose wealth. If you don't invest for the good life then what you will have is poverty, failure, and misery. Failure and poverty is like a default or an automatic setting. You must make a choice and plan for wealth. But, if you choose poverty you don't have to do anything just work and spend all your money and you will have poverty, regrets, and misery in your later life.

In America, the corporate owned news media has conditioned us to believe that wealth is only reserved for the top few. The media defines the term wealthy to mean that you must have a net worth of a million dollars or that you must have millions of dollars sitting around in the bank. With this definition, the average citizen deems wealth unattainable. So, we say what the heck, with this definition of wealth I could never be wealthy and free. So, we just give up, work for 40 years, earn on average a million dollars, become a consumer, and give the system our money and we get credit cards only to create our very own poverty. But you see this is not our definition of wealthy. What if you can change this definition or reframe it to suit you. To guarantee that you can make yourself wealthy you must change the definition of wealthy. Instead of thinking of a pile of money as the definition of wealthy, think in terms of an income that you need to live your lifestyle. You can see this is a much smaller number than millions of dollars. The truth is wealth is personal, it's simply a steady stream of income that you don't have to work for. It's just that simple, nothing more nothing less. You are wealthy when your personal resources produce enough income to pay your expenses without you working, simple, and achievable by anyone.

FACT: YOU WILL EARN A MILLION OR MORE OVER YOUR WORKING LIFE

Earning more money will not solve your money problems,
keeping what you earn will

It's simply a myth to think that you don't earn enough money. Yes, you will most likely earn a million or more over your 40-year working life. You can do this with low wages or in some cases minimum wages. This is what the system knows and we don't. *We all know how to earn money; we just don't know how to keep it. So, we think that we should get a second job to earn more money. Only to end up with less, because the taxing governments will take more of what we earn. And what they leave us, we spend buying more stuff that we don't need.* We must learn how to keep what we earn first, and use this money to make us wealthy. Then we can earn more if we choose.

They know that we are all millionaires running around out there without the proper training on how to use our money to make us wealthy. Therefore, the system job is to take most of it from us, and you know they do. We have not done the math on our lifetime working wages. They know we are not taught to value our money. We think the sole use for money is to buy stuff instead of putting it to use to become financially free. This is what we ultimately want to be free and enjoy our lives and not worry about money all the time. **So how do we become millionaires**? *Let's break this down. How will I become a millionaire with my measly income?*

Well if you earn on average over your 40 years working life $12.50 hourly before tax, you will become a millionaire. What you say $12.50, that is a low or minimum wage? Yes, I call this the $12.50 millionaire plan. You will see the power of small amounts of money and time. If we just earn a low wage, we can still become millionaires. If you move up to management or get married you will most likely multiply your millions.

Most people believe that the definition of rich or wealthy is a million dollars. So, let's start there at a million dollars and perform some math on your life time million dollars. The typical amount of hours that we work every year is 2,080. If we back out the vacation, two weeks or 80 hours because not every employer pays for vacation days for hourly employees then we are left with 2,000 hours.

I worked at a plant for 10 years and the plant workers were paid hourly with unpaid vacation time. However, we all work 50 weeks of the year. Finally, if you work a typical 40 hour week, you have a total of 2,000 hours of work each year, over your 40-year working life.

So, start with a million dollars since this is your goal:

You will earn a $1,000,000/40 years working life = $25,000 yearly.

Divide your $25k by 2,000 hours =12.50hr.

So: $12.50 X 2,000 hours X 40 years = $1,000,000

Yes, all you need to earn is $12.50 an hour and you can become a millionaire. Pretty cool huh? You will earn a million dollars over your 40 years working life by making minimum wages of $12.50. And let me suggest that most Americans earn more than $12.50 hourly. According to the Labor Department's Occupational Employment Statistics. In the U.S. all-occupations had a mean salary of $47,230 ($22.70 hourly). So most of us will make double our million.

In addition, if you move up to supervisor or management levels you will earn many more millions over your working life. So we all are millionaires. This is what they know that we don't that's why they end up with our money and we are reduced to poverty depending on social security and Medicare to help us and of course we paid for that too. If I gave you a million dollars, I believe that you will find a way to manage it well. However, because you get it in small amounts you cannot see the big picture. But they – the system can, take a look.

SO WHERE IS YOUR MONEY?

Look no further than the system: banks, insurance companies, mortgage interest and taxing governments. They have your money. We are all little millionaires running around here doing what they told us to do to get the American Dream and yet we just can't seem to get ahead. We are doing all the work but just can't seem to accumulate any money. Why? Because you are playing, buy the system rules. The system writes the rules so they can win, and they are winning. So, if you continue to follow their rules of the system money game, you will lose. The system deals in consumer debt and taxes. **Their rules are for you to be a consumer**. The system needs consumers, people just like you to buy their worthless depreciating junk and pay taxes on it. They get your money and you get to feel good for a couple of days until the monthly payments start. Then it's back to work to earn more money to buy more crap. We do this repeatedly and we teach our children and they do this repeatedly until we all die. Folks we can't win like this. It's time for some new rules. If you want to win the money game and keep the money that you earn to make you wealthy, then you must play by a different set of rules. A set of rules that will put you in the winner's circle. This book will show you how to change the rules in your favor so you can win. So, you can have a chance to become wealthy, not them.

Keep in mind that if you follow the majority, 95 out of 100 people will be either dead or dead broke at age 65. Four will be financially independent and only one will be rich. In the richest country on the planet only 5 people out of 100 will ever be financially free to do what they want when they want. Think about that read this again. This is not my study it's the governments. Then look around you and you will see this all around you so it is true, but it does not have to be true for you. Let's change this for you starting right where you are with the money you are earning right now. Let's discuss the major theft of your money.

WHY AREN'T WE WEALTHY?

We certainly earn enough but we can't seem to keep it and we certainly don't use it to make us wealthy. In fact, as you can see we do just the opposite. We unknowingly use our money to make other people rich.

Look what happens to our million:

You earn a million dollars:	$1,000,000
One third goes to all taxes:	(333,333)
One third goes to paying interest payments:	(333,333)

You have a third left:	$333,333/ 40 years
	= $8,333

You get $8,333 a year to live on. To raise your family, go on vacations pay health insurance, save for your children's education and save for your retirement. This is not Mexico, Cambodia, or North Korea; this is America you can't live off that little money! However, this all you get! No wonder we are all broke. Our lifetime millions are literally being stolen from us by the system. The same system by the way that told us how to spend our money.

Now can you see what's going on here? This is a very simplified calculation. It's worse than this I just wanted to make you think that you are going to have some money left over. Student loans are more than ONE TRILLION DOLLARS according to the Fed!! Because the poor and middle class cannot afford to pay for their children college costs and neither will you. Well in order to plug the holes in our finances we have to find the leaks.

Keep in mind that wealth or financial security is simply a steady stream of income that you do not have to work for. You are wealthy when you can live comfortably off the income that your assets produce without you having to work, period. So you don't need a million dollars in the bank to be wealthy. What we need is the asset the produces the income. Wealth is all about money working for you not about you working for money. When I ask many people what makes them wealthy? They would say a million dollars in the bank. I would tell them that a million dollars locked up in the bank will not make them wealthy. Why, because it is not generating income for you. Now if you take that million dollars and buy 10 rental homes at $100,000 each and you can rent them for $1,000 a month each, now your million dollars will be generating $10,000 a month income enough for you to live comfortably. You still have the million dollars it's just been move to assets that produce income for you. This is a practice that I have been following for years. I would convert as much of my money as I can into rental homes or assets that pays me income so I don't have to work for money if I don't want to. This is freedom of choice.

THE TAXMAN COMETH

"The hardest thing in the world to understand is the income tax."
– Albert Einstein

"If you drive a car, I'll tax the street, If you try to sit, I'll tax your seat. If you get too cold I'll tax the heat, If you take a walk, I'll tax your feet."
—The Beetles- Taxman

"The government's view of the economy could be summed up in a few short phrases: If it moves, tax it. If it keeps moving, regulate it. And if it stops moving, subsidize it."
--Ronald Reagan

Taxes, Taxes, Taxes: Folks the biggest expense that we will ever have in our lives is not our mortgage, but taxes. Taxes will take just about 50% of all the money you will ever earn. However, I will use 33% because I want you to think that you will have a chance. We need to get together and **CUT THEM OFF (CTO)**! If you are going to have any chance at freedom, you have got to get a handle on your tax bill. Study this book to give yourself a chance. If you don't find ways to legally slash your taxes you won't have a chance at the American dream which is financial freedom. This is my song: I go to work to earn my money and they taxed my dollars. I spent my dollars and they taxed it again. I tried to save my dollars and they taxed that too! Here are some of the taxes that we pay. To stop them we must become tax efficient we will discuss this in a later section. This is just a small summary:

SMALL SUMMARY OF ALL THE TAXES THAT YOU PAY:

Federal Income Tax, Social Security Tax, Federal Unemployment Tax, Medicare Tax, Gift tax, Soda/fatty-food tax, Alcohol tax, Ad Valorem Tax, Alternative Minimum Tax, Bank ATM transaction tax, Building Permit Tax, Kiddie tax, Driver's License Tax, Cigarette Tax, Corporate Income Tax, Tax on imported/exported goods, Estimated income tax underpayment penalty, Dog License Tax, Excise Taxes, Fishing License Tax, Food License Tax, Fuel Permit Tax, Federal Gasoline Tax, State Gasoline Tax, Yacht and luxury boat taxes, Gross Receipts Tax, Hotel/Motel Tax, Hunting License Tax, Federal Inheritance Tax, State Inheritance Tax, Liquor Tax, Gas/electric bill fees & taxes, Marriage License Tax, Water/sewer fees & taxes, Personal Property Tax, Real Estate Tax, Rental Car Tax, Service Charge Tax, Hotel/Motel Tax, Road Usage Tax, Sales Tax, Recreational Vehicle Tax, Education School Tax, State Income Tax, Local Income Tax, State Unemployment Tax, Federal Telephone Universal Tax, Federal, State and Local Surcharge Taxes, Telephone State Tax, Telephone Local Tax, Telephone Usage Charge Tax, Utility Taxes, Vehicle License Registration Tax, Vehicle Sales Tax, Watercraft Registration Tax and Well Permit Tax.

This list is not complete there is a lot more Tax, Tax, Tax. Let's CTO!! No wonder you can't get ahead and if you don't turn this around, well, I hope you love eating cat food in your retirement because that's all you're going to have. Later in this book, we are going to show you how to give yourself a tax break, because you need one. You must educate yourself if you ever expect to have anything. Let's go on and talk about the next silent thief.

DEBT INTEREST PAYMENTS

The inability to delay gratification. This is the mindset of the poor. They want it now, so they go into debt to get it, only to realize that when you use debt and credit cards to get it now you are really creating your very own poverty. You are stealing money from your future. Because you will have to use you future income to pay to have it now. Consumer debt robs you of your future.

Folks there are entire industries out there are all involved in this easy credit scheme, from the banks to the department's stores to the governments that allow them to charge us 20% on credit cards. The politicians are in it because the US economy is all based on credit and debt. The GDP measure all goods and services sold in the US and almost all of this is paid for by credit and debt. Heck, the government owes $20 trillion. We are going to CUT THEM OFF- CTO. Get rid of these people. They literally will get you hook on credit. Yes, credit is an addiction just like alcohol, drugs, cigarettes, caffeine, and many other addictions. We will talk more about getting free and breaking our addiction or habit to credit and its ruthless destroyer of families called debt interest payments. Paying interest on bad debt like credit cards and car loans etc., makes you poorer. But, good debt that is the debt to buy assets that appreciates in value or pays you a return that covers the interest payments makes you rich. So not all debt is bad we will discuss this later in the debt section of the book.

Yes, I know you have heard this before but we must say it again. You must begin to wait until you can afford to pay for certain items and save money on interest payments. We want it now and so the credit peddlers have made it very easy for us to go into debt forever, they even make it sexy: "What's in your wallet?" What in your wallet is debt? The question is not what's in your wallet we know what that is? The question is what should be in your wallet and that's cash not credit cards! Try it carry some cash around and see how it make you feel. Credit cards make you poorer. They want you to believe that a wallet full of credit cards will make you look cool, not just any credit card but: Gold Cards, Platinum Cards, hell they even have the ultimate Black Card. They all do the same thing: rack you up with a load of bad debt. You don't need to wait any more the marketers say. No need to wait until you can afford it they say! You should wait until you save the money to buy the depreciating items that you just don't need. But what's in your wallet? The goal of the banking institutions seems to be to stick a credit card in every man, woman, child, and unborn child's pocket just so they can suck money out of your life forever, and you know they do it. I had several credit card offers when I was in college and I had no income. I had no education on how to use credit so I thought it was free money. I burdened myself down with debt and later in my young life, I went bankrupt. I had no idea what I was signing up for and the small monthly payments added up and crushed me like a bug. Lesson well learned.

Below is an example of the effect on your life time earnings of $1,000,000, if you buy a bedroom set of furniture marked down from $7,000 on sale to just

$5,500 you will save $1,500. Wow what a deal you say! So you reach for that credit card and make minimum payments because you did not save up any money and you think this is a good deal so you want it now! Talking about going broke saving money look at this:

Credit Card Balance $5,500
Credit Card Interest Rate: 18.9%
Minimum Payment: $200
Years to pay off balance 11 years 4 months
Total payoff $8,109.16

Now does this sound like a deal to you? What happened to the $1,500 saving? Instead, of getting the discount of $1,500 you paid an additional $2,609 of pure interest that you get zero benefit. So you pay them $2,609 just for the privilege of using their $5,500. This is not 18.9%. Folks the real interest rate is almost 50%. Fifty percent interest, look at it again! This should be against the usury laws in this country. But these loan sharks have found a way to get around the laws. These credit card sharks should be in prison wearing a striped suit with big numbers painted across their chest while they make license plates for the rest of us.

ADOPT THE MINDSET OF- PAY AS YOU GO

You must operate 100% on cash for consumer purchases, no debt, pay as you go! The lesson here is to save cash to pay for the items you want to purchase. In the above example the only difference between you enjoying a saving of $1,500 and paying an additional $2,609, is cash money not credit, cash. **Cash is still king!** This is why big business takes your cash and give you credit. The more you use cash the more you can take advantage of bargains like this. Now you will have to take this $2,609 out of your future earnings. So consumer debt makes you look good and feel good now. Immediate gratification, but in the end you are getting poorer not wealthier. Consumer debt does not enrich your life at all and I hope I just proved that to you here. The fact is that you know we make lousy deals like this every single day using credit cards. The rich get richer and the poor gets stuff that depreciates or go down in value such that they become worthless. If you are going to turn this around, then you must do simple math and learn to use cash to get deals not credit. Even if your practice is not carry a balance on your credit cards, I would recommend that you pay with, cash or debit card. With credit, you will have to pay interest payments that have nothing to do with the purchase. There are many calculators on the web for you to do your own analysis.

Mortgage Interest: Consider the effect of purchasing a home on your lifetime $1,000,000 earning. Now I realize that most of us including myself went into debt to purchase our homes. I just want you to be aware of the effect of debt on your lifetime earnings. Keep in mind that your lifetime earning is just a number. You will earn so much money over your working life and that will be it. So the closer you are to estimating that number and what is happing to your life time earning the better you will be at determining what to buy and how to best to pay for it knowing that your life time earning is limited especially if you work for an employer. I believe that purchasing a home is your biggest asset. I say asset because to me if something goes up in value over time that's an asset and that's what I want to own. But since its consumer debt we have to lump it here. So here goes:

Say you need a loan to buy that beautiful home that you saw. The value of this home is $105,000 but you can buy it for $100,000. So you run to your local friendly bank to qualify for the loan. You have a job and excellent credit so you get the money. Keep in mind that low interest rates can often push you to buy too much house that you just don't need. You have a family of three and yet because of low interest rates you can qualify for a 7-bedroom house, but you don't need a 7 bedroom house. So you buy it anyway because you can qualify for it. So why is your friendly local bank just dying to help you? Because they love you? No! They know you are going to pay a ton on interest and make them rich!! According to www.Zillow.com the median price of homes listed in the United States is $214,900, February 2015. Ok for simplicity, we will just use $100,000. You can run your own numbers later. I just want to prove a point here, not give you a heart attack, stroke, or something. Ok here we go:

Home Price $100,000
30 year 6% mortgage
Interest payments $115,838
Total payments $215,838
Total tax paid 33%

So you have to earn $287,118 because you have to pay the government 33% in taxes or $71,226. That's almost $300,000 or almost 3 times the price of the home just to pay the friendly folks at your local bank $115,838 in interest just for a $100,000 mortgage. This is just principal and interest not taxes, insurance or fees etc. If I add taxes and insurance, I know you will stroke out for sure, so let's keep it simple here. Now wait a minute does this sound like a friendly deal to you? No. I just want you to start to look at the total payments that you will be paying using credit and its effect on your lifetime income of $1,000,000. You see this $300,000 comes out of your $1,000,000 lifetime earnings. Ok now do you see why you don't have any money or why you can't seem to keep any of it? I mean it comes in and goes right back out the door, and if you don't stop it you will retire flat broke depended upon the government to save you. We will talk about the social security that you will be depending on later in another section. But for right now look at these numbers again. Look at your mortgage papers and see the total amount you will pay. Look at the total cost of things that you buy on credit, not just the monthly payments.

RULE #2
START THINKING
AND ACTING LIKE
THE WEALTHY

THE FINANCIAL HABITS OF THE WEALTHY

"Money makes money. And the money that money makes,
makes more money"
B. Franklin

THE MINDSET OF **the wealthy is to: pay yourself first, save, invest then spend.** The investor consumes as well however, they understand that you cannot spend all your money on consumer items. Their main focus is to save and invest a portion of their earned income from a job into assets that goes up or appreciates in value and produces a steady stream of income for life so they won't have to work for money. This is the path to the real American dream, financial freedom. For me I chose the path of rental real estate because I understand the business and I have a talent for it. Others have chosen to take a portion of their earned income from a job, and invest in a retirement plan, and still others have created a business of their own in their spare time. When the business becomes profitable, they simply hire a manager or a family member to manage the business for them. This will relieve them from the day-to-day management of the business. Since you know the profitability of your company, you can simply request that they send you your share of the profits as dividends from the business while you are vacationing on a beach in Hawaii sipping one of those cool, cold, funny looking drinks with that little colorful umbrella in it.

We will discuss several other ways to invest for income in the later section. As an investor, I am only interested in making my investments pay for the depreciating consumer items that I want. The investor begins their career just like most of us by working at a job, the difference is that the investor mindset causes them to turn the income that they earn from a job to unearned income or passive income. The investor is interested in making money work for them instead of them having to use their most valuable limited asset, which is time for money. The investor is interested in freedom and they know that the only way to have that is to buy income-producing assets. These assets will pay them income forever without them having to work for money. When you purchase this book, your investor mindset kicks in and asks, how is this book going to provide value into my life and provide me a return for my investment? Now you have adopted the mindset of the investor and not the consumer.

WHAT IS WEALTH?

Wealth is a steady stream of income that you don't have to work for. You are wealthy when you can live comfortably off the income from your own personal resources without you working, period. So, you don't need a million dollars in the bank to be wealthy. What we need is the income that your wealth produces. Rental property, annuities, dividends, interest payments, right down to your social security payments. All income, all wealth.   Wealth is all about making money work for you so you won't have to work. Many people believe that wealth is a million dollars in the bank. They know they will never have a million dollars just sitting around in the bank so they give up on wealth creation and go to work to create wealth for others. The truth is that a million dollars locked up in the bank is money but not wealth. Why, because the money is not generating income for you.

Now, if you take that same million dollars and buy 10 rental homes at $100,000 each and you can rent them for $1,000 a month each, well, now your million dollars will be generating $10,000 a month income, enough for you to live comfortably for life. This is wealthy. You still have the million dollars it's just been move to assets that produce income for you for life. What this means for you is that if you need $2,000 income monthly and you have 2 rental homes or a mixture or annuities and social security, it doesn't matter, if you can live off the income from your personal resources you are wealthy.   This is the truest purest pathway to prosperity. You can turn your lump sum 401k or IRA savings into a steady stream of income for life without working as well. Awhh, the American dream at last. As Warren Buffet said: *if you don't find a way to earn money while you sleep, you will have to work until you die.*

SPEND LESS MONEY THAN YOU EARN

To keep what you earn, you must start by spending less money than you earn. I know you have heard this before but I am going to repeat it: Spend less money than you earn and save. **If you save money, then money will save you.** This is a basic law and is the most violated by the working class. **Following your money is the only way to keep it.** I am not saying go on a strict budget and live in a cave like a monk. No, far from it, but what I am suggesting is that you discipline yourself to set aside a certain amount of money from your paycheck just to invest and make yourself wealthy. The working class earns money and simply spends their way to poverty. It's not what you earn that counts but what you do with what you earn that counts. What you do with your money counts, and it's all a choice. You can choose to use it to make yourself wealthy and escape the rat race or you can use it to spend your way into poverty. American consumers are in $11 trillion of consumer bad debt because of violating the principle of spend less than you earn. If you are not willing to spend less than you earn and save, then close this book and give it to a relative or friend so they can make themselves wealthy because you will never be free. If you can't save because of all the bad debts that you owe, then we will cover this in the get out of debt section of this book. But for now, spend less than you earn and save.

Remember the mindset and habits of the poor is to spend first then save what's left. But the problem with this spend first then save poverty mentality, is that there is nothing left to save, so they remain poor. But, if you do the exact opposite and adopt the mindset and habits of the wealthy which is to save first then spend. Well you can see that this will put you on a path to freedom. SAVE FIRST: Start saving now! This is where you get to decide how much financial freedom means to you. This is your first step. Put yourself first no matter what. Make a commitment. A lot of people that I personally talk to tell me that: *"David I can't save any money, I spend all I make, I am simply not making enough money"*. I tell these people that if you can't afford to save then you can't afford to spend because ultimately this will end in your poverty. If you don't have any money then you must go into debt and that does not solve your problem, it is the cause of your problem. You must live below your means for now. You must cut back on your spending. There are only two ways to have more money at the end of the month and that is either to expand the income circle or reduce your expenses. That's it! You must understand that debt is not your problem, you are the problem because you refuse to become a good steward of your money. You become a good steward when you make a decision to pay yourself first, *"Save first then spend"*. Having access to capital is good if used correctly. But when you consume your capital you are sliding down on a slippery slope to poverty and living a dependent life style, dependent on the government your family and friends to support you.

PAY YOURSELF FIRST!

To keep what you earn is a mindset, it means to pay yourself first! To save a portion of your income first before you pay anybody else. The IRS knows the importance of being paid first so they take their share of your paycheck first. You get to live on what's left. Maybe the government is trying to show you the importance of putting yourself first. This is your new mantra: Pay yourself first! The new rule for you is to save early and often. Why, because money buys freedom. Freedom of choice. Without choices, your freedom is limited. In America, no one is going to give you freedom. You must act now, I don't care if you set aside $10.00 a month do something. I suggest start with your next paycheck and save no less than 10% into your local bank account just to get the habit of it. Paying yourself first is the best way to develop good habits and begin to change your habits from a poor person to a wealthy person. This is such a powerful basic principal but it is the most violated by most working Americans. Studies have found that 76% of Americans live paycheck to paycheck with zero savings. How else can you explain the fact that people work their entire adult lives, 40 to 50 years earn a million or more and end up with nothing. Paying yourself first is simply thinking long term. It's setting aside at least 10% first out of every paycheck before you pay everybody else. This is best performed by having your employer automatically deduct at least 10% from your biweekly paycheck and invested into a saving account or better yet a 401k or IRA.

YOU WILL NOT GET A COMPANY PENSION!

You must create your own pension. You can do this by simply investing in things that goes up in value and pay you income. Most of us are fearful of retirement because we have no money. We go from working our entire lives to poverty. Why? Because we did not pay ourselves first. Currently you must work 8 hours a day, 5 days a week, 50 weeks a year for 40 years and your employer will not give you a pension. All you get is all you've saved. Keep in mind that when you stop working the money stops, savings, health care and life insurance all stops! Start thinking and acting like an investor. You must invest your savings in things that pay you income for life.

YOU MUST UNDERSTAND THAT YOU ARE IN A FINANCIAL WAR!

There are executives dressed in nice suits sitting in boardrooms strategizing on how to take as much of your money away from you that they possibly can. And, you know what, they do it. They get our money plus interest and we get poverty and the crippling burden of debt. It's time for a change. We are going to turn the tables on them. It looks like a conspiracy of the big banks and departments stores to give a credit card to anybody with a job and a pulse. It's their mission to stick a credit card in the hands of every man, woman and child in America and you know what they almost do it. If they can give your new born infant child a credit card before they leave the nursery they would do it. Then the marketers aim is to sell you a bunch of crap that you don't need, but you think that you do. Next, they stick that credit card and siphon hose into your pocket for the rest of your life just siphoning as much of your money away from you as they can and it's all legal!

These people are criminals that should be behind bars dressed in black and white striped clothing with big black numbers printed across their chest. The only job that these credit cards prostitutes should have is making license plates in prison for the rest of us. Yea, *"what's in your wallet?"*

WHAT IS FINANCIAL SECURITY?

"the first duty of man is not to be poor"
George Bernard Shaw

My definition of financial security and wealthy is the ability to live off the income from your own personal resources without working. In other words, peace of mind. This is a choice. Remember wealth is a choice. When you are wealthy and financially secured you do not have to live with the constant threat to your well-being such as a loss of income from a job. In other words, you have a steady stream of income coming in to meet your expenses without you working. All your basic expenses that you need to live comfortably and worry free are secured. Now, if you lose your job then the creditors can't come and take your life and the things that you have worked for away from you.

Once you achieve financial security you can go to work because you want too not because you have too. There is a big difference here as I personally discovered.

This is easier than you think. If you have not attained financial freedom, it's not because it's impossible, anything is possible, but because you have not chosen financial freedom as a goal or a priority that you want to achieve. This is the number one reason that the poor and middle class do not achieve financial freedom it's because we simply do not plan for it. We never believe that financial security and freedom is a possibility for us so we don't even think about it. And of course, we wake up one morning in our future at 65 years old, sick, and broke with no income coming in. This is the sole purpose of this book to instruct you on how to achieve this covenant title of financial freedom the American dream, get it before it's too late.

PLAN FOR FINANCIAL SECURITY

"I expect to spend the rest of my life in the future, so I want to be reasonably sure what kind of future it's going to be. That's my reason for planning."
C. Kettering

Do you ever think about it? What's your plan for your future? Where are you going to be say in 5 years, 10 years, 20 years from today? This is the problem with 97% of us Americans, we simply don't plan. Planning for your future is the difference between waking up early in the morning at your retirement age and having to go to work at Walmart as a greeter or you can be on vacation in the Caribbean Islands on a white sandy beach sipping mojitos. It's your choice. You must immediately develop a plan and care enough about it enough to create an urgency within you to see its fulfilment.

Keep in mind that you are in a war, a financial war! The banks big business and the taxing politicians have teamed up to take as much money away from you as they possibly can. Don't believe me then look at your bank account. Where is the money? You work for it and they steal it! Hey, the politicians bailed out the banks and big business during the financial meltdown of 2008, which they caused through their greed. Remember, big business and the banks got richer and you were stuck with the 19 trillion-dollar tax bill. So if you don't learn how to bail yourself out then who is going to bail you out? Do you know that you will earn a million or more as an employee? Wow, you are rich! Well let's see how rich you are. Ok where is 75% of all the money that you have earned? Ok where is 50%? Ok how about 25%? Where is 10% of all the money that you have earned in your working life? Think about it. They get your money and you get the credit cards and make debt payments for the rest of your life! Let that sink in for a moment.

Planning: Yes, we are going to talk just a little about the importance of having a vision a dream a plan and setting goals to reach them. You see planning is the magic elixir, it's a road map. Moreover, if you don't know where you are going any road will get you there...to nowhere. Planning one's life and goal setting is another subject that is not taught in school and this is why we are failing in our lives because we don't know where we are going. I am talking about written goals. To me a plan is not a plan unless it's written down somewhere. I have my life plans nailed to my bathroom walls right over the toilet and the mirror. So every time I go to the bathroom and look in the mirror I know exactly what I should be doing, and so should you. This is true happiness because I know where I am going every day.

To demonstrate the importance of goal setting and planning, in the seventies a group of Harvard Graduate Business School, MBA students were asked: have they set clear written goals for their future and have they made plans to accomplish them? The study found that only 3% had clear written goals. Ten years later the same group was interviewed and they found out that the 3 % that had written plans had more money than the 97% combined. Need I say more about planning and goal setting? I think you get the picture.

If you are going to win this war and you want to live your life on your terms, you have got to have a plan. A plan is a specific date that you want to have a specific sum of money or income that means that you have won. This is your freedom number, or freedom fund. Once you have an amount of money that you need by following the system in this book, you will be able to convert this plan into a three-phase wealth creation system. By the time you reach phase three you will be well on your way to creating wealth in half the time. This system will allow you to practically automate your wealth creation plans. In other words, set it and forget it. Keep in mind that a plan is a specific amount of money that you need to live your life on your terms. No wealth will come to you unless you plan for it. A plan is the *"Why"*, this is the energy that you will need to see yourself through to the finish line. We will discuss more on planning as we go along in this book.

WITHOUT A PLAN, MOST OF US LIVE OUR LIVES WITHIN THIS POVERTY EQUATION:

Income – Spending = Saving.

The problem with this equation is that there is nothing left over to save.
For five days we spend all of our mornings and evenings earning money just to give

it all away, we spend more than we earn we have nothing to save so we go into debt with credit cards. Sounds familiar? If you were a business the equation would be Sales – Expenses = Profits. If the expenses are larger than the sales you go out of business period! Same with the family equation if your spending is larger than your income you go into debt and bankruptcy. You will not create any wealth. **If you want to create wealth and money, you must rearrange this equation to look like this: Income – Saving = Spending**. You will have to save first then spend. You have to be committed to wealth creation while you are able because there will come a time when you will not be able to work to earn money. **Your Financial Plan equation: Financial Goal + Spending = Earning**. So if you need $15,000 as a down payment on a house and you're spending $20,000 you need to earn $35,000. That's it. So, the question becomes: *"how can I earn $35,000?"* Add more value and you will earn more money. This is how it's done period. You get the $15,000 for the down payment for the home and you begin to create wealth from thin air through inflation, which causes an increase of equity in your home, and your net worth will grow. You use this net worth to create more wealth and wealth creates more money and on and on.

There is no amount of money that you cannot out spend. So you will need a plan and commit to it and you will have it. This is how it's done. Which means that the first skill needed is discipline not budgeting just mental discipline to take 10% right off the top before you pay anybody you must pay yourself first. That is why I am suggesting that we start our journey with saving a small 10% of your gross paycheck. You should increase this amount necessary to reach your financial freedom goals. You can arrange to have this amount automatically deducted from your paycheck and sent to your retirement plans or bank saving account, not a checking account. Later we will talk about more investments ideas that will offer you greater returns, income and tax sheltered growth. Since money seems to be a problem for the majority of us let's talk money.

BECOME YOUR OWN FINANCIAL EXPERT

YOUR PERSONAL ECONOMY IS ALL THAT MATTERS!

You become your own financial expert when you learn how to control your consumer debt and invest your money in things that goes up in value and pays you income. There is only one reason to invest your money, and that is income. This leaves you with very few choices to invest your money. Knowing this makes you the expert. We will outline the only investments that creates wealth and income at the same time in his book. Keep what you earn and use it to make yourself wealthy. Stop thinking and acting like a consumer and adapt the investor's mindset. Whether, this country's economy is going through an inflation, deflation, stagflation, recession, or a depression, none of these economic cycles should keep you up at night! I have heard that a recession is when your neighbor loses his job, a depression is when you lose your job. You do not have to participate in any of these economic cycles if your personal economy in your home is booming and growing. **As long as you have emergency cash in the bank and your investments are growing, compounding tax-free, paying you interest and income then, who cares about this rubber band global economy**. This is what you are going to learn in this basic money course. It's time for you to start looking out for yourself and your love ones because no one else will. That's what this money course is all about, financial freedom. Your personal economy is all that matters and it's your responsibility. Notice that the global economy can be booming and growing but if you are drowning in debt and can't pay your mortgage then your personal economy is in a depression. So take control of your personal economy today because that's all that matters.

To do this you must read this book and become your own financial expert. Becoming an expert means that you have researched all ways to reduce your expenses so that you pay for only the services that you need and want. Create a spending plan for yourself. I call this planned spending project the 20/50% solution. That is, you should research all expenses and reduce your normal expenses like: life, auto, and health insurances by 20 to 50%. Cut your credit cards and department store interest payments by 20 to 50%. Cut your utilities and I phones, WiFi Cable TV expenses by at least 20 to 50%. These expenses are the reason you can't seem to accumulate any money. The only point that I am trying to make here is that if you want to keep the money that you earn and use it for your freedom then you must take control of your finances now. Become your own financial expert. So get on the phone, make some calls, and reduce your increasing expenses.

WHAT IS THE PURPOSE FOR MONEY IN YOUR LIFE?

The purpose of money in your life is not just to consume stuff but to help you live your life according to your values. Your values are attributes about yourself that makes you feel wealthy, happy and fulfilled. If financial freedom is something that you value, then the purpose of money in your life is to help you become wealthy and financially free. This is living a wealthy lifestyle. If you ask this question: *what is the purpose for money in your life?* to the next one thousand people that you see, most if not all of them will draw a blank stare. We have never been taught to think in terms of the purpose of money in our lives. Therefore, we live our lives in mediocrity in quiet desperation doing what everybody else is doing and we go to the graveyard with our song still in us after working 40 to 50 years, just like everybody else. If you don't master the principal of "spend less than you earn" then just put this book down because your life will have a limited purpose and you can never be free.

Freedom is the American dream and you deserve a chance to achieve it. Once you sit down and think about your true values then you must align your money with your values. If you do not do this exercise, then you could be spending money buying stuff that has nothing to do with your true values. The result will be a much-unfulfilled life. You must examine how you are spending your money to determine whether you are living consistent with your values, if so you are probably happy and feeling fulfilled.

Obvious putting a high priority on your short-term value of "fun and excitement" while not planning for your long term value of "security" will inevitably be a problem for you in your later years. I worked with a personal coach during one of my counseling sessions and she asked me to write down the 10 things that I value the most. At the top, I wrote down freedom. When she saw this she asked me, if you value freedom the most then why are you working 12 hours a day doing tax returns? Well I had no answer for that. However, I finally realized why I was so unhappy, I was not living my values.

Now, since this exercise worked for me I am going to have you write your top 3 to 5 true values down and see do they make sense for your whole life. To know the purpose of money in your life, you will have to know what you value the most then you can answer that question. Your values may be different from your love ones, which may be causing the conflict in your relationships.

If I ask you to write down 3 to 5 of your most important values what would they be? Ok I am going to ask you to turn the page and list them. But before you go I **don't** want you to list goals. A goal is stuff that you want or stuff that you buy. If you want $10 million dollars this is not a value it's a goal. The value may be that you crave "power". Another example: you may want to be able to take a walk in the park with your spouse in your arms every day at 12:00 noon. This is a goal, your value maybe "A loving marriage"

You should create one sheet and have your spouse or significant other create a separate sheet listing their top 3 to 5 values. Then compare the list to see if you have differences that are causing any conflicts in your relationships. Because, if one of your top five values are "security and safety" with a goal of saving $100,000 and your spouse is" fun and excitement" with a goal of vacationing in Hawaii for 6 weeks 4 times a year at a cost of $100,000, that's going to be a problem and there will be conflict because you are not spending your money according to your values and purpose. Therefore, by making a list of your values and comparing them you can plan how both of you can reach your truest values, goals and be happy. The purpose of money in your life will be to facilitate these values or lifestyles.

On the other hand, if you are forced to spend money that is not consistent with your true values, then this probably explains why you are frustrated and angry. Once you have made your list of values then look at how you are spending your money. Are you managing your money consistent with your true values? If you don't look at this you will reach the end of your working years only to be depressed because you bought a bunch of stuff and lived your life in a manner that was not consistent with your true values.

WHAT IS THE PROPER USE OF YOUR MONEY?

The proper use of your money is to live debt free, prosperous and retire wealthy. This means being a good manager of the money that you work for is the proper use of money. But how do we do this, no one is teaching this stuff, thus we often spend more than we earn and make poor investments choices that funnel our wealth into the hands of our creditors, taxing politicians, and wall street crooks. I have taught on the subject of money for a long time and have always said that there is only a hand full of things that we can do with money. You can borrow money, lend money, earn money, spend money, give money, save, and invest money. Can you think of anything else? If so, please tell me. Therefore, if you are having money problems chances are that you are over extending in one of these areas.

To manage your money well you must know how much you earn, how much to borrow, to loan to spend, how much to give, how much to save and how much to invest. No one talks about this! They say that most people will not talk about money because it's personal and emotional. Well, most people are broke! They are broke because **no one ever taught them the proper use of their money**! The system only wants you to work for money and spend your money to keep the economy going as they tax you to your grave and into your next life. The system will have you ending up with nothing and cannot even retire and enjoy a decent life. Don't believe me, go to Walmart and see who greets you at the door, retirees! Don't laugh because unless we educate ourselves financially this is going to be our future.

So let this brief discussion be the beginning of your financial education. If you are going to keep money, you will have to learn how to manage money. The magic is that when you become a good steward of money then you will be blessed with more money. Keep in mind what the good book says: *to him that have more shall be given..."* This means that the rich will get richer and the poor will get nothing. We want you to become one of the rich. This is so important because how you manage your money is very important, it will determine the most important areas of your life like, what type of car you can drive, whether or not your children will go to a private school or to a government provided public school, what type of clothes you will wear, where you will live, right down to the bottle of wine that you drink and the brand of shampoo that you use on your hair. Being a good steward or money manager will cut across every area of your life.

Therefore, I just keep this simple. Being a good steward of your money should be simple not complicated. I just pay myself first. I save and invest a full 30% of my income mostly in things that appreciate and produce income for me, and the rest 70% is subject to meeting my current daily planned expenses. I keep it simple. Maybe this will work for you. You can use 20% saving and investing and 80% expenses or whatever combination that works for you, just do it, and commit to it. Nevertheless, you should be saving and investing at least 20% at a minimum. We will talk more about this later. I don't really care for strict budgets or tracking every penny because it's not fun and it takes too much time. So, if you make budgeting to strict just like counting calories on a diet, you will not stick with it. I like to enjoy my life. I play basketball and golf in my spare time. However, I am educated financially and you will be to by the end of this money course book. Remember wealth is a choice, poverty is a result from not making that choice. Choose wealth.

THE INDEPENDENT VS DEPENDENT MINDSET

Currently in America, only 5% of the people can live off the income that their personal resources produce. A full 95% of Americans cannot retire and live an independent lifestyle. They have to be dependent on the government or a job to take care of them. In America, only 5% of the people are independent and 95% are dependent. You need to take charge of your own life and your own retirement plan so you can be in the 5% not the 95%. Are you living the life style of dependency? A dependent lifestyle means that you are not keeping what you earn. In fact, you are using your money to make other people rich and not you. Are you using your money to make others rich? A dependent life style also means that you are currently living your life spending all or more than you earn creating a mountain of debt and not creating any wealth. If you are living like this then you are living a dependent lifestyle. The result is that you will always be dependent on a job or the government or someone else to take care of you in your later years. Being a greeter at Walmart is your true destiny. You will have to work not because you want to but because you have to. This workbook will show you a better way.

Are you living an independent lifestyle meaning that you are building or have sufficient assets that will pay you a check that you don't have to work for? An independent lifestyle means that you may be still working but you are creating wealth so you will not have to depend on a job or the government or anybody to take care of you.

In this section, you will be able to determine which of these lifestyles that you are currently living and if this is not what you want to continue then you can change it starting today. Up until now you have probably have never realized that the financial results that you are now receiving is due to the path that you have chosen or your current mindset, either the mindset of the consumer or the investor. This mindset probably is a result of your paradigm. It's the surroundings that you were born into and as a result it becomes the lens that you view the world and what is possible for you. So If you were born into a home of lack or middle class then you will have to break out of that type of thinking that is holding you back before you can reach the wealthy or rich class. America is the land of plenty.

Our state of mind controls and direct our entire future and if you want to have a different future outcome then work on your mindset first. You must come to realize that you have the power to control and direct your destiny here in America. No other country on earth has this protected constitutional power. You have it! Since our lives comes from how we think, once we see where we are going and decide to make some changes then our results will change for the better. As you begin to think about a more prosperous life something will happen within you and you will begin to seek a more prosperous life and you will find it. Keep in mind that in American we can choose the economic class or lifestyle that we want, either (very poor, poor, middle class or choose to be wealthy and rich). It's all about how much value we decide to add using our talents to enrich other people lives. You have heard the saying: Find a need and fill it. I heard it once said that we can get what we want by helping others get what they want. So, we can change our current status by simply educating and developing our God given talents to add more value than anybody else and we will be rewarded in kind. This is the law of cause and effect or sowing and reaping. On the other hand, if we don't choose the economic lifestyle that we want then the system will choose the lifestyle for us and that is to work like slaves spend all of our money to make others wealthy and rich not us. So, let's see where you are on the financial economic highway.

You Are Here		LIFE STYLE ECONOMIC LANES THAT YOU ARE TRAVELING ON				This is where You Are Going
Economic Lanes	Income comes from	Expenses	Liabilities	Savings	Investments	Life style
Very Poor Class	Government	yes	no	no	no	dependent
Poor Class	low pay Job/ Government: Earn Income	yes	yes	no	no	dependent
Middle Class	Higher pay Job/ small business: Earn Income	yes	yes	yes	401k/IRA/Pension	dependent
Wealthy/Rich Class	Investments: portfolio, passive income	yes	yes	yes	401k/IRA/Pension Income producing assets	Independent

THE LANES EXPLAINED

Very Poor Class: This class is a starting point for a lot of working class Americans. It's where we start from and pull ourselves out from this class. This class is economically and financially dependent 100% on the government for food and healthcare social programs administered by several Federal and State assistance programs for the poor and low income Americans. They have expenses, mainly food to feed their children. They have no liabilities because they can't get loans to buy cars and other stuff. They have no saving and no investments because they have so little income from the government that they spend all of the money that comes into their household on expense items like food and utilities. They are not taxed. In 2014, domestic food assistance programs served approximately 25% of Americans. The government spent a total of $103 billion on these social programs to help feed 46.5 million Americans that received food stamps. The poor receives on average from the government $103 a month. This class gets its money from the government, state and federal social Medicaid programs for the poor. The Medicaid program is a social health care program for low income or no income families. In 2014, the Medicaid expenditures were about $449 billion for 65 million Americans. The people in this class are living a dependent lifestyle and are dependent on the government for their income and support. If they do not move out of this class they will be dependent on the government forever.

CHANGING LANES FROM THE VERY POOR TO THE POOR CLASS:

To change lanes on this highway to a better class, Americans must seek to educate themselves. Education is the ticket out for the very poor and the poor. Low wage jobs are possible however, to move out of this class they should graduate from some type of high school or trade school. Then they can move to the Poor Class.

The Poor Class: The people in this class may still receive some assistance from the government's social programs but they are not dependent on these programs for 100% of their income. They may have minimum wage jobs while they climb their way out of poverty by going to night school community colleges, trade schools while receiving education loans and grants. They have expenses, few liabilities and no savings or investments because all of their money is going to pay for expenses mainly food to feed their children and healthcare cost. In fact they qualify for what is called a negative tax meaning that through the income redistribution process they can qualify for the "earned income tax credit". The government takes from people that pay taxes and give the money to the poor class. So the poor pays no taxes and yet they can qualify for a refund. People that are in this class are currently living a dependent life style and unless they move out of this class, they will be dependent on low paying jobs and the government social security programs forever.

CHANGING LANES FROM THE POOR CLASS TO THE MIDDLE CLASS:

To change lanes on this highway to a better class, Americans must seek to graduate from these improvement schools, community colleges then go on to State colleges using education assistance loans and grants. They may want to start a small business as well. Through their efforts, they can get a better job and better pay then they will move to the middle class.

The Middle Class: This class is a step up from poverty. This class is a victim of the inability to delay gratification. They pay their bills on time and therefore have good credit rating and so the marketers sell them on buying stuff that they don't even need. This is the cause of most people never moving out of this class because they create so much debt that all of their time is taken up working just to pay for the depreciating items that they buy. However, there is no official definition of middle class as it relates to income because $50,000 will go far in Oklahoma but it will not get you anything in New York or California. So for the most part the people in this class are well educated, have businesses, may be a two income house hold earners with 2 1/2 children and a barking dog. This class has mortgages debt, other liabilities and all the trapping of wealth but it's mostly smoke and mirrors because it's mostly debt from the shoes on their feet to the food they eat is purchased with a credit cards.

The middle class may have higher incomes and higher expenses and liabilities but they are starting to save and invest their money mainly in their employment pension plans i.e 401k/403b/457 or IRAs as well. These retirement plans can become income producing as well, however they rarely have enough saved in these plans to produce the required income that will allow them to retire comfortably. But the middle class through these saving and investing plans have begun to use their money to make them wealthy. They also have regular pay raises and can change jobs seemingly at will for higher pay. The American dream at last...so they think. Even though they have higher incomes and investments and saving accounts they are still living a dependent life style because they are mostly 100% dependent on their incomes from either their small business or their employer. Get comfortable here because this is where the majority of Americans will spend their lifetime. They may find it difficult to move to the Wealthy/ Rich class because they are spending their 40-hour weeks working at a job. Limited time is a problem for the middle class. This class will pay the most in taxes as a percentage of income than any other class. They will spend up to 50% of their income paying taxes, which keep them in the rat race, and going back to that job forever. This class is living a dependent life style because they are dependent on their jobs 100% and maybe social security to help provide enough income in their retirement.

CHANGING LANES FROM THE MIDDLE CLASS TO THE WEALTHY CLASS

To change lanes on this highway, the middle class must stop being consumers and become investors. They must learn to convert their earned income into assets that produces income for life without working. An asset that produces unearned or passive income is the true definition of wealth. These types of investments i.e. rental property are taxed preferred so your wealth will grow much faster.

The Wealthy: Financial freedom is the goal of this class. They have mastered the ability to delay gratification, the secret to becoming wealthy. This class fully understands how to use their money to make them wealthy. They have expenses, liabilities, and maybe high incomes from a job. They possibly have some funds in retirement plans whether it's an employer plan, small business plans or individual plans. However, they have purchased assets or own businesses that produces income for them so they don't have to work. They may pay the least in taxes because their investments are usually tax preferred. Meaning they may pay zero taxes for their real estate because of the allowable tax deductions. They may pay capital gains taxes on other investments. They do not pay social security taxes on these types of investment incomes because they are considered unearned income, which is not subject to the same taxes as earned income from a job that you pay. You have heard of billionaire Warren Buffet talks about the unfairness in the tax law that allows him to pay lower taxes as a percent of income than his secretary. That's because his income is considered unearned income, which is taxed less than earned income.

To understand this class you have to get a definition of wealth. Wealthy or financial freedom is a steady stream of income from assets or investments that pays your lifestyle expenses that you do not have to work for. Being wealthy is not the same as being rich. You can be rich on paper, say you have $10,000,000 worth of gold locked in a bank vault but it is not providing you income so you have to go to work to earn income to pay for your expenses. You are not considered wealthy or financially free until your assets can produce enough income to pay for your lifestyle expenses whether it's $2,000 a month or $2,000,000 a month. You are not considered wealthy or financially free until your asset produces enough income to pay your expenses. When your assets produce you enough income to pay your expenses without you having to work then you are wealthy and financially free to do whatever you want with your time. This class is living a 100% independent life style.

THE LIFE STYLE OF POVERTY

Most Americans are taught to live a life of dependency. From birth, we are dependent on our parents, then as we grow up and enter the public-school system we are prepared to become dependent on a job and the government. We are taught to work, pay taxes, and rely on social security for retirement. This plan makes us 100% dependent on the government for our financial support and leads us to a life of poverty. Below are some of the attributes of a dependent person

- They spend more than they earn.
- They max out and have balances on credit cards.
- They buy things that depreciates in value: cars, clothes, I phone etc.
- No plan to be wealthy
- They do not develop themselves and learn new skills to improve their income.
- They spend time they do not invest time.
- They become dependent on the very thing they hate, their jobs.

THE LIFESTYLE OF WEALTH

They start out as a baby very dependent on their parents. These people go to the same schools and are taught to be dependent on a job and the government just like the dependent life style person. However, they began to look around and see that no one is winning the money game just working to make other people rich. The politicians through increasing our taxes are getting rich. Why else would someone spend $600,000,000, almost a billion dollars to become president just to have the privilege of earning $400,000 a year in income? The independent person realizes that the CEOs and shareholders all are getting rich off his talents. He sees that the department stores and the banks are all getting rich except him. Therefore, the independent person understands that they have to increase their financial knowledge and learn how to use their money to make them wealthy. They need to learn how to make money with money instead of working for it all the time.

These people have figured it out to be wealthy you must become a creator of value. The more value you add to the most amounts of people the more you will be rewarded and become wealthy and rich. If you want more money then add more value become a resourceful person. The universal law is value equals wealth. Money flows to the person that makes life easy for everybody else. Remember that your job here is not to create money. Your job is to create massive value, and the value creates the money.

The independent minded person realizes that if you want millions of dollars then find a way to add value to millions of people. If you want to be a billionaire add massive value to billions of people. Bill Gate-Microsoft, Mark Zuckerberg-Facebook, and Steve Jobs- Apple to name a few – dropped out of college prior to achieving fame and fortune. They figured it out if you want to be rich then add massive value to billions of people and you too will become rich. The secret to Wealth is to become a creator of value. I have added value in writing this book. I add value by offering my rental homes for people to raise their families and they in return pay me rents. Your status in life is directly proportional to the amount of value that you have been adding to people. The seeds we sow today bring forth the abundance and wealth we receive tomorrow. Below are some attributes of an independent person:

- Self-development via education and training.
- Self-starter business owners.
- Buy assets that appreciates in value and provides income.
- Depends on themselves.
- Consider ways to add value to receive additional income and rewards.
- Self-motivated and responsible.
- Very dependable.
- Constantly seeking ways to improve themselves.
- Have enough income to share with their favorite charity.
- Community leaders.
- Takes full responsibility for their health.

PHASE 1:
CUT THE EASY CREDIT OFF

EASY MONEY AND DEBT

THE CONSUMER DEBT PROBLEM IN AMERICA

Americans spend all or most of their income on
things that have little or no lasting value!
-Thomas Stanley

PLEASE DO NOT pass go on this section. Americans spend first then save what is left. The problem is that there is nothing left to save. We have too much month at the end of the money. If you are not willing to spend less than you earn and make this a priority then you can never be free. You are part of the problem. Do you know that according to the U.S. Bureau of Economic Analysis: Personal Savings in the United States is in decline from an averaged 6.80 percent from 1959 until 2014, reaching an all-time high of 14.60 percent in May of 1975 and a record low of 0.80 percent in April of 2005 right before the financial meltdown 2007-2008? Personal Savings in the United States increased to 4.90 percent in December of 2014 from 4.30 percent in November of 2014. This is basically due to the scare of the entire financial system meltdown in 2007-2008. People are afraid and don't trust the financial system. I know I don't.

However, this section will reveal the results of us citizens spending more money than we earn. Look below and see what we are contributing to. This is where our wealth is. And if we don't make a commitment to becoming financially free then our only alternative is to continue to add to those horrible stats on the next page. If you are not willing to comply with this principal: *"Spend less than you earn"* then just close the book right now because you will have sentenced yourself to a debt sentence for life. This is the most violated principal in America by the poor and middle class. They simply spend more than they earn, they spend first then find that there is nothing left to save. So, they remain vulnerable to the same financial system that failed them in 2008. To make up for the cash short fall because they are not putting saving first they reach for the fairy cards, the make-believe money cards you know your *"Master"* cards and Visa cards. Yes, they become your master and you are the slave because you will be working for them forever.

The average household has $15,611, in credit card debt that's almost a third of the $52,250 annual medial income for the US according to the Census ACS survey for

2013. Also, according to a bankrate.com survey, 76 percent of Americans are living paycheck to paycheck. This simply means that the first sign of financial disability or an interruption in their paychecks they will have no other recourse but to start missing monthly payments and there we go into bankruptcy or financial default. Yea what's in your wallet? Well take a look next to see what's in your wallet:

WE THE PEOPLE ARE IN A LOT OF CONSUMER BAD DEBT

*As of June 2016

U.S. household consumer debt profile:

- Average credit card debt: **$15,657**
- Average mortgage debt: **$177,341**
- Average auto loan: **$27,865**
- Average student loan debt: **$49,591**

In total, American consumers owe:

- $11.45 trillion total debt
- $729 billion in credit card debt
- $8.36 trillion in mortgages
- $1.26 trillion in student loans
- $1.1 trillion auto loans

*According to Nerdwallet.com an analysis conducted by the Federal Reserve statistics and other government data:

According to an article by Fox Business published May 14, 2014, the US Median American Savings is $0. The typical American isn't saving anything, even though we have the capacity to be tucking away extra funds each month. So what's going on here? Let me sum it all up. We are making money at median income of $52,250, we have savings of $0 dollars or very close to it. So we are not saving at all, and we have a debt load of $11 trillion. What does this tell you? We are not being good stewards of our money. We are living a dependent lifestyle depending on the government services to bail us out. We are horrible at saving money which means we are going into debt just for normal daily purchases like food as well as emergencies.

Since we don't have any money we have to go into debt which prompts the banks and Wall Street to keep coming up with cute ways for us to go into debt. The bank sees this data and they know we are not in the habit of saving money so they pick our wallets. They make going into debt seem normal and sexy *"what's in your wallet'?* I'll tell you what's in your wallet, maxed out credit cards.

We the people are literally drowning in debt. Look at our leaders of the greatest country on earth our government they can't help us they are a large part of the problem. They are drowning in debt. The government could never pay off its debt and they don't intend to they don't have to because they got you to pay the interest for them through higher taxes and eliminating some of your tax deductions. What a deal, they spend and you get to pay. They just keep borrowing money that they create from nothing. Because as the deficits rises they tax us more so we bring less home to save and invest for our future so we see no other recourse but to follow the leader our government and go into debt. The deeper the better for the banks but not for you.

Like we said earlier, the government is not a household and they don't have to pay back debt as long as they can get you to pay the interest through higher taxes. So, listen up it's time to turn the table around. But the only way to beat them at their debt game is to adhere strictly to this principal: SAVE FIRST – SPEND LAST! Complete opposite of what you have been doing. The majority of us has been spending first and saving what left and you see there is nothing left. We keep buying the latest I-phone and other apps and gadgets we don't even understand how to use them. Let's dig out of debt fast and get in a position to become the bank ourselves. Yes, you become the bank and loan them money make them pay you interest. Buy their stock and make them pay you dividends and gains. Loan them money let your money make you wealthy instead of giving it to them. This is called the turn around and this book is designed to do just that turn the tables around on them so they will make you wealthy. How is that for a change? OK let's take a look at how our government leaders is managing our money.

THE USA NATIONAL DEBT

The Outstanding Public Debt as of 2 December 2016, at 12:06 am
$19,910,036,390,445
The estimated population of the United States is **324,996,749**
So, each citizen's share of this debt is **$61,264.**
The National Debt has continued to increase an average of
$2.19 billion per day since September 30, 2012
U.S. NATIONAL DEBT CLOCK

Basically, the National debt is the total amount of debt owed by our federal government. The $19 trillion amount includes the money that is borrowed and the compounding interest as well. The government will borrow money when it doesn't collect enough money from taxes, and fees to pay for its social programs like the military, the national parks, etc. But this debt will continue to grow larger and larger. As long as our economy keeps growing then the government can keep borrowing forever. But this does not matter to you because unlike your household the government does not have to pay its debt because it will not go into bankruptcy like you can. It doesn't die it lives forever. See the clock above each of us citizens share of that debt is $61,264 for every man woman and child. So, if you have a household of four that means your household owes $245,056. Wow!

HOW THE NATIONAL DEBT DIRECTLY AFFECTS YOU:

Consumer Interest rates: One of the ways that the National debt can directly affect you is by rising interest rates. The currently low rate of the Treasury bonds actually acts as a benchmark for consumer loans like your mortgage interest rate, credits cards, car loans even your student loans, basically all consumer loans. So the lower the Treasury bond rate the lower your consumer rates will be so pay attention to these rates. There, I just gave you a reason to watch the Nightly Business News.

Higher taxes: At some point, the National debt will have to be paid down at least. The options are to raise your taxes again or eliminate some of the social and entitlement programs that we all enjoy, plain and simple so beware.

PAY OFF YOUR MONEY SUCKING BAD DEBT FIRST!

CUT THE MONEY SUCKING CREDITORS OFF!

The goal is to cut these money sucking creditors off before they destroy your life! Use the money that you were throwing away making debt interest payments to make yourself wealthy, not them! If you have bad debt, then let's **Cut them off!** Get completely out of this unproductive and destructive bad debt. In fact, *cut up these cards except one! But do not cancel or close out any of these cards as this may negatively affect your credit rating. You must pay them off first then get rid of them. If you must keep one, then choose a debit and a cash back credit card. The debit card is tied to your bank account so you can't get into trouble here.* The reason I said keep one is because our society is set up to use credit cards, just try to make a hotel reservation or rent a car without one. But for now, we are going to cut up all cards and put them in your dark closet in a shoe box. Later these cut up cards will remind you of the source of your misery. The number one reason you must cut up these credit cards is because you want to break your borrowing addictive *"crack-cocaine"* like bad debt habit! You want to cut off all sources of debt from coming into your life right now. The secret and the fastest way to get out of this crippling debt is to focus all your attention on the remaining balance not the interest rate. The only way that the banks can charge you interest is if you have a remaining balance.

Example: if you owe $5,000 of credit card debt at 19% interest rate this will cost you $950 in interest payments your first year. If you pay off the balance it's like getting a GUARANTEED 19% return on your money and getting a $950 return of your money! When I figured this out it was amazing!! This alone gave me the energy to pay off my bad debt. Just do the numbers yourself. You are getting a 19% return on your money GUARANTEED! Now where else can you get that type of guaranteed return in today's financial markets? If you find a guarantee like this please let me in on it. Let's cut them off now!

"Something that is instantly gratifying will be repeated"
Steve Wynn

To become free of bad consumer debt you must learn to delay gratification! I want it now! For now, we will just get rid of the blood sucking credit cards. Your credit score will be increased automatically without you doing anything but paying down the balance. Say if you have a mortgage with a high 8% interest rate because of your bad credit, once you pay off your cards your credit score (FICO) will increase. Then, you can refinance your mortgage at a lower rate. Use your money to make you wealthy! Use this saving and put that into your wealth freedom fund to make you free. You see these guys are stealing your future your very own freedom from you! Credit cards does you no good it's not real money. Credits cards make you think that you have real money. Steve Wynn the creator of the billion dollar Las Vegas gambling casinos and hotels empire, made billions by understating human greed which is at the base of our psychology.

He quoted the secret to his success *"Something that is instantly gratifying will be repeated"* That's it and he, the banks, mortgage companies and credit card drug pushers are making billions off you. This is what he said about your inability to delay gratification. It is time to realize your own psychological state when it comes to credit cards and CUT THEM OFF!! If you want a better tomorrow, a more prosperous tomorrow if you want to ever be free then you must cut them off today!

THE REAL SECRET TO ELIMINATING DEBT FAST!

The quickest way to become debt free, and to eliminate all of your debt, including your mortgage in the shortest time possible is to focus all of your extra money to paying off *your outstanding principal balance only.* Do not make any extra interest payments. Make sure that your extra payments are being applied to reducing your principal balance. Remember no balance no interest charges no monthly payments. Oh what a relief that is. You cut the debt suckers off by eliminating the principal balance that you owe! From this day forward when it comes to your debt, I don't want you to focus on the interest rate, because the banks will determine that. You cannot control the rate they charge you. What you can control is eliminating your outstanding balance.

Example: A $1,000 principal balance with a 12% simple interest rate will cost you $120, a year just in interest payments no principal here in this calculation. The principal part of your monthly minimum payments is estimated to be just 2% of your monthly payment. Therefore, your high interest rate is not your problem it's your large outstanding balance.

Example: $0 balance x 250% interest rate = $0 interest payments.

Got it? You need to look at your balance the principal balance and focus all of your energy on eliminating this principal balance. *"No balance no payments"*. Simple! The creditors goal is to hold that balance on you as long as they can. They want you to pay the minimum payments forever. Let's use a technique to get rid of our bad debt. Start today.

MY PERSONAL PROBLEMS WITH CONSUMER BAD DEBT

I had an easy money credit spending problem. This mentality drove me into a bankruptcy court at a young age. I learned that I had to break the habit of spending so much money on depreciating assets. Like big flat screens TVs, pool tables, fitness equipment, corvettes, brand name clothes suits and shoes. I was literally jumping head first into an ocean of debt just to impress people that I didn't even know. I was trying to impress my neighbors who I didn't even like and they didn't like me. And I was going into debt trying to show these people that I was well off. What a fake I was! I was literally getting up before sunrise, going to a job that I hated. Driving thru traffic that I hated, going to a place to work that I hated, to be ruled by bosses that I did not like and they did not like me only to turn around and do the same thing the next day. At the same time while I was driving to work I was scared to death that I was going to be fired!! No kidding this was my life for years. I lost my job, could not make the minimum payments and the creditors forced me into bankruptcy. I lost everything. What a lesson I learned.

Finally, I said enough I will do whatever it takes to get out of here. And I began to look at all the stuff that I had that just was not making me happy but was keeping me poor and returning to that slave life that I was living. I took some steps to reduce my expenses, and sold the crap that I did not need nor wanted and put all the money to a saving and debt reduction plan. The money I received for my sales I called it "Bonus money". This is the money that I would start paying off my debt. My Bonus or the money I made from my garage sales was $2,100. I paid off some of other debts and use the $200 that I had left to start a mathematical pay off process that will guarantee that I will be able to pay off my bills as fast as possible saving thousands in interest payments. This is how I did it.

You can sell something or whatever to find some extra money to start your payoff. If you have more expenses than income they you have two choices either reduce your expenses or sell something to start the payoff. Then list all your debt on this debt management sheet on the next page. Next you can choose any payoff priority you want. Make it fun. Or you can do what so many others have done and simply start paying off first the debt that has the highest interest rate. Or you can start the payoff with the smallest balance first. This will make you feel good because you have eliminated your first debt. I chose the highest interest rate to get started. The whole idea is to eliminate the principal balance because without a balance they have nothing to charge you interest on. Got that? It's the balance that is your problem not the interest rate, but the balance. This is what you are eliminating. Fair enough? Ok let's go look at my sample. There are several variations of a debt elimination table all over the internet but this is the one I developed that helped me to manage my bad debt and raise my FICO score at the same time.

HOW TO ELIMINATE YOUR MONEY SUCKING BAD DEBT

1. List all of your debts that you want to reduce or eliminate on the Debt Management Sheet per the example on the next page. Remember if it's good debt meaning debt that is used in business and is generating profits for you and the interest is 100% tax deductible then don't include these business debts. However, get rid of bad debt.

2. Next apply any bonus money to start your payoff. Look at my example, I list my debt using the highest interest rate first. Ok then I applied my bonus money to that debt first. Then after I paid it off, I just applied the payments to my next debt that I wanted to eliminate.

You can see as you pay off your debt the monthly payments will get bigger and bigger as you roll from one debt pay off to the next until all debt is eliminated. Now when the debt is paid off or manageable for you then we will use this extra money that we were wasting to make debt payments we will use it in the next investing section. We will use this money to invest in assets that goes up in value not down and that produces income for you.

FICO scores: Paying off bad debt has its rewards. Your FICO score should increase after each major payoff. Use this Debt Manager to manage your FICO score. If you want to repair your credit for the purchase of your first home, then you should research the credit scores needed for this type of purchase. As you pay down your bad debts, monitor your FICO scores as well to ensure that it reflects your new status. You are then able to use this new FICO score to acquire productive good debt. The kind of debt that pays you money. In addition, as soon as you get your FICO score elevated then you can request to refinance your loans and credit cards to a lower interest rate as you continue your payoff process. That's why this process is a debt manager not just a debt payoff system. We will discuss FICO scores in the third section.

EXAMPLE: # MY DEBT MANAGEMENT TABLE

Creditor whom I owe	My Balance Due	Interest Rate	Minimum Monthly Payment	Minimum Payment plus Bonus	Pay off	Results of Debt Management Process	Wealth created from interest savings	FICO
Student Loan	$ 20,000.00	12%	$ 220.00	$220 +200=420	1	Paid off	$ 3,757.00	680
Credit Cards	$ 5,000.00	11%	$ 98.00	$98 + 420 = 518	2	Paid off	$ 1,451.00	700
Car loan	$ 17,000.00	8.50%	$ 395.00	$395 +518 =913	3	Working		
HDTV	$ 2,170.00	5%	$ 115.00		4	Pay Minimun		
Pool Table	$ 1,300.00	4%	$ 57.00		5	Pay Minimun		
Gold Clubs	$ 750.00	0	$ 55.00		6	Pay Minimun		
							$ 5,208.00	

I recommend that you visit this website and use their financial calculator at: *http://financialmentor.com/calculator/debt-reduction. This calculator will calculate your savings, which is very important.*

Go to *Appendix Section "H"* for a blank form you can make as many copies as you need.

THE TURN AROUND!

Can you see the magic? I was paying off my debt at a pretty good rate. I had an extra $913 that I created to continue paying off my debt. That is amazing. Look at my savings of $5,208 that I had saved instead of giving my money to the banks. Noticed that I did not go out and get another job to pay off my debt I use the money I already earned to become debt free. At this point, my savings was $5,208 and I had $913 just to invest in assets that will pay me income. Now that we have a pile of money that we created, let's use it to invest to make us wealthy instead of them. Notice at the same time I raised my FICO score which I used to get into good debt.

FOLLOW YOUR MONEY

THE CASH FLOW STATEMENT

"You can't eat your cake and keep it to"

To keep what you earn and to become financially free, you must start right now to follow your money. How can you keep some of it, if you don't know where it's going? The answer is the Cash Flow Statement. This is how you keep what you earn and follow your money. Cash is King! Managing your cash flow on at least a monthly basis will determine whether you become poor, go nowhere, or become wealthy. To learn how to manage your cash flow and to know where to invest your surplus cash can make you financially secured for life. The rich, poor and middle class all starts here. The Cash Flow Statement. If you are spending more than you earn, then there is absolutely no way to create wealth and freedom for yourself. Remember that the habits of the poor are to spend all that they earn and save nothing.

Listen, if your income remains the same but your expenses increases the money must come from somewhere and this is the reason that your credit cards balance keeps growing. By the time most people track their cash flow they will find that they are way over their heads in debt because of spending more money than they earn. Once you can face your current cash flow problems and make the necessary changes to get in alignment with your income and goals, suddenly your world will look a whole lot better.

To become financially secured for life you must spend less than you earn and invest the difference in assets that produces income for life without you having to work. I have also included a "Before, After and Change column". You can use this cashflow statement to make changes to your expenses or income. You can also use this Cash Flow Statement to determine what your finances will look now and changes you must make for you to stop working or retire, whatever. But what is most import is that you make changes that will ensure that you have a positive cash flow because this is the money that you will invest to make yourself free and wealthy.

To get started you will need to gather all of your sources of income and expenses. If some of your income and expenses occurs on a quarterly, semiannually or annually basis you can spread them out over a monthly basis. Say if your health insurance is paid quarterly then you must break that total down to monthly amounts. We want to measure all income and expenses monthly. This is a short enough period for you to make some adjustments. Your goal is to create positive cash flow. You will use this money to create an emergency fund and financial security for yourself.

Please take a moment to complete the Cash Flow Statement on the following page. I have included a copy in **APPENDIX SECTION - A in the back of the book.** Feel free to make as many copies as you need.

CASH FLOW WORKSHEET

INCOME	BEFORE	AFTER	CHANGE
My take home paycheck			
Spouse take home paycheck			
Government			
Pension/Retirement			
Investments			
Other			
TOTAL MONTHY INCOME			

EXPENSES

CATEGORY	EXPENSE	BEFORE	AFTER	CHANGE
ESSENTIALS	Food			
	Clothing			
	Medical			
	Education			
	Child/Pet Care			
	Other			
HOUSING	Mortgage/Rent			
	Utilities			
	Phones			
	Maintenance/Repair			
	Other			
TRANSPORTATION	Auto loan payments			
	Oil/Gas/parking/tolls etc			
	Other			
ENTERTAINMENT	Dining			
	Cable TV			
	Internet Service			
	Other			
INSURANCE	Life			
	Home			
	Auto			
	Medical			
	Other			
INVESTMENTS	Bank/Cash			
	401ks/IRAs			
	CDs			
	Brokerage			
DEBT	Credit Cards payments			
	Personal loans payments			
	Student loans payments			
	Other			
	TOTAL MONTHLY EXPENSES			

CASH FLOW STATEMENT	BEFORE	AFTER	CHANGE
TOTAL MONTHLY INCOME			
subtracted			
TOTAL MONTHLY EXPENSES			
equal TOTAL MONTHLY CASH FLOW			

YOUR INCOME AND EXPENSE

This section is only used if you want to analyze a more detail track of how your cash is flowing. What comes in vs. what goes out. Knowing what to do with the difference can make you wealthy and free or plunge yourself into the deepest debt of poverty. If you are ever going to be financially free, secure and live the American dream, you must know your numbers. Follow your money! So, let's take a moment, sit down with a cup of tea, and create your very own prosperity, your own future. Understand that unless you learn how to use the bank's money to make yourself wealthy and free, what you will create is a mountain of consumer destructive debt. And you and you alone must pay what you owe plus interest, to get yourself out. Destructive debt will negatively impact the rest of your life.

So, let's get started with your expenses and liabilities because this is the lifestyle that you are living. The question is, are you borrowing to support these expenses or are you earning enough income to support your current life style? *Preparing a Personal Expense and Income Statement is your very best defense against financial worries.* It will make sure that you stay on track to keeping what you earn. It's like x-ray vision allowing you to consider the future and see problems before they happen so you can take corrective actions. All big businesses prepare monthly financial statements to see where they are headed financially and that is why they remain successful. Most people never see how they are doing financially until it's too late. They have a mountain of debt that they no longer can afford the monthly minimal payments and their lives are changed for the worst.

TABLE 1- LIVING EXPENSES/MONTHLY

Please note that your Living Expenses should not include any installment debts other than your mortgage. The total of these expenses will provide us a rough estimate of your personal living expenses. Your saving or emergency funds are excluded from this expense listing. You can use the back of this page to add more line items to this listing as well. We are just trying to get a major break down of your expenses. Look at your "miscellaneous", you may want to itemize this section to see exactly what you are spending your money on. These are your statements so do with them as you please. So turn the page and get started.

Table 1- Living Expenses/Monthly

Mortgage/ Rent payments

    (include taxes, insurance

    dues etc.) $_____

Groceries $_____

Utilities (phone, electric, water etc.) $_____

Insurance (health, life, auto) $_____

Medical (prescriptions, doctor visits) $_____

Transportation (gasoline, oil, taxi, buses, fees) $_____

Child Care (school, support etc.) $_____

Miscellaneous expenses $

    TOTAL $_____

Go to APPENDIX SECTION "B" for a blank form make as many copies as you like.

LIABILITIES (INSTALLMENTS DEBTS)

Next we will look at your Liabilities or "Installments" Debts. This will give you a good ideal as to where you are creating interest payments that are slowing down your financial freedom date. We have a section on how to rapidly eliminate these debts in the following sections. If you feel that you may miss some creditors just get a free copy of your credit report from https://www.annual**creditreport**.com. Let's get started.

Table 2 - Liabilities (Installments Debts)

Name of Creditor	Minimum Monthly Payments
	$
	$
	$
	$
	$
	$
	$
	$
	$
	$
	$
	$
	$
	$
	$
TOTAL	$

Go to APPENDIX SECTION "C" Liabilities (Installments Debts) Table 2. You can make as many copies as you like.

MONTHLY INCOME STATEMENT

Next we will look at all of your income from all sources. These items total listed should be after tax. I want you to list your take home pay. I realize that you are paid every two week so just multiply by 2 and list your monthly income.

Table -3 Income

Sources of Income	Monthly
My take home Paycheck	$_____
Spouse take home Paycheck	$_____
Support /Alimony	$_____
Tips	$_____
Government (unemployment, etc)	$_____
Pension/Retirement	$_____
Part Time	$_____
Military	$_____
Commissions	$_____
Passive/Investments/Savings	$_____
Other (Welfare, family, etc)	$
TOTAL INCOME	$_____

This will be our first step to financial freedom. So, let's first see if our monthly cash position is either positive or negative. This will give you a very good picture of how you have been managing your personal finances.

Go to APPENDIX SECTION "D" Table 3 Income Statement for a blank form make as many copies as you like.

Table 4 - Summary Table

Finally let's compile these totals into one easy read table

Total "Living Expenses" from Table -1	$_____	A
Total "Installment Debt" from Table -2 +	$_____	B
Total of Living Expense plus installment Debt	$_____	A + B
Your Income from Table -3	$_____	C
Total Cash Flow "Subtract (A + B) from C for positive/negative cash flow"	$_____	

Go to APPENDIX SECTION "E" for a blank Summary Table make as many copies as you like.

Is the "income" Table-3, greater than that of the combined "Living Expenses" from table 1 and the "Installment Debt" from Table 2 total? IF the answer is "yes" then this is good because we have some money to invest for your financial freedom. Also, next we will complete a "Personal Net Worth Statement". This will show you how you have been spending this extra money, so read on.

   If the answer is "No" we have some work to do to solve this problem. We have two options here and that is either to expand the income circle or we need to eliminate some of our installment debts and expenses.

YOUR NET WORTH IS A STATEMENT ABOUT YOU

A personal net worth statement is like a personal financial fitness checkup of you at a snapshot in time. It's just like your annual physical fitness exams that you receive from your doctor. Based on the results of your examinations; weight, blood work, cholesterol levels, heart rate, glucose levels etc. The doctor can tell whether you have been taking care of your health or not. Well a Net Worth Statement tells you if you have been taking care of your financial health as well. The biggest thing your net worth statement reveals is your disciplines and commitment to your own personal financial freedom of choice. Remember wealth is a choice poverty is the result of not making that choice. Your Net worth is just a simple straightforward equation: Assets minus Liabilities = Net Worth. You can perform this anytime simply by subtracting your liabilities from your assets at a specific moment in time. This will determine if you have a positive net worth or a negative net worth. If you find that you have more assets than liabilities, you have a positive net worth. If you have more liabilities than assets, your net worth is negative. This is not all bad but it just shows you where you are in your overall goal attainment of financial freedom.

Your mission is to work towards a positive net worth, this can be done by simply paying off some of your debt if you have a negative net worth. Many people may have a negative net worth, but that can be due to normal debts like student loans, mortgage debt, and credit cards etc. This may be normal when most people are just starting out on the road to financial freedom. The net worth statement is a good compass that points you to where you need to focus.

So, when you examine your net worth statement you may see that the student loans are a big portion of your net worth then you can simply make a spending plan to reduce this liability by allocating a larger portion of your debt pay off plan to this debt. We will discuss a way to manage your debt by using a simple straight forward "Debt Freedom Plan" later in this section. But, view your net worth statement as a work in progress looking for areas where you can improve. Basically, the goal is to have a positive net worth. I recommend that you perform a new net worth statement annually then set a goal for where you want to be, say you may want more cash in your saving account for emergencies to equal 6 months of your basic expenses. Then this is a perfect tool to review monthly or quarterly to see if you are on track.

HOW TO CALCULATE YOUR NET WORTH STATEMENT

You can simply make a list of all your assets. These are things that you own that has some monetary value like your cars, home, your furniture cash in the bank, all stocks account all pension funds, art work your jewelry basically anything that has value you just get all of those documents together and simply make an estimation of the value. You can call a local realtor and inquire about the value of your home. Don't worry about perfection at this stage.

Next, you do the same for your liabilities. I suggest that you get a copy of your credit report. This report will list all of your total debt balances not just the monthly payments. We want the total liabilities here. List all of your mortgages, student loans, and back taxes that you may owe. Include all credit cards balances, and medical bills. Make sure you include money that you owe because these are your liabilities.

Ok view this example below, just remember the formula: Assets (things you own that have monetary value) subtracted from your liabilities (debts that you owe) = your net worth. Assets – Liabilities = Net Worth. Here is an example below:

ASSETS

Checking account	$2,100
Emergency saving account	$3,250
All other banks accounts	$1,125
Home market value:	$197,000
Car market value (wife):	$12,000
Car market value (husband):	$8,000
Pension 401k account (husband):	$22,000
Pension 401k account (wife):	$15,000
All IRAs accounts:	$2,600
All other investment accounts:	$2,000
Total Assets:	$265,075

LIABILITIES

Mortgage:	$190,000
Student Loans	$54,000
All credit cards	$21,000
Car loan (wife):	$2,700
Car loan (husband)	$11,700
Owe Parents	$9,500
Total Liabilities:	$288,900

(Assets) $265,075 – (Liabilities) $288,900 = negative net worth - $23,825. So, our net worth here is a negative $23,825. This means that our family here has $23,825 more in liabilities than they have in assets.

USE THE RESULTS TO MAKE SOME IMPROVEMENTS

One of the many purposes of creating a Net Worth Statement is to be used as a budgetary guide. You can spot where you need to make some improvements i.e. the student loans and credits card. You may want to create a spending plan that will allocate more funds to eliminating these debts or maybe you want to sell the wife's car and use the money to pay off the credit card debts or student loans. Money can ruin a good relationship. However, since your parents do not charge you interest you can maybe pay them later. We will discuss this in our Debt Freedom Plan Section.

Ok next exercise let's complete your Net Worth Statement.

Note: Remember that a net worth statement is just a snapshot of the current value of your financial holdings at a point in time. Beware that the market value of your assets can change drastically. So, it's a good idea that you should update your net worth statement at least once a year during tax season. This is where you have to give an account of your earnings anyway, so this is an excellent time to update your Net Worth Statement.

Go to APPENDIX SECTION "F" for a blank Net Worth Statement make as many copies as you like.

HOW TO MEASURE YOUR WEALTH

There are generally **two ways to measure wealth**: Net Worth and Passive income

1. **Net Worth:** Discussed in the Personal Net Worth Section. Just a reminder:
   Assets – liabilities = Net Worth
   Assets (things that you own)   minus
   Liabilities (debts that you owe) = Net Worth
   Net Worth. This can be positive or negative. If positive, then you should put this positive net worth to work for you creating more cash, income, and wealth for you.

WORKSHEET

Things to remember | **Actions To-Do** | **Dates**

2. **Time:** The next way to measure our wealth is in time. Wealth is not only measured in net worth or money in the bank but by time. Your wealth is measured from the time you stop working until the time you have to go back to work to pay your bills. If your passive income is greater than your expenses, then you are financially free and you don't ever have to look for a job to pay your bills ever again. This is your goal. The reason why you want to measure your wealth in time is because you want to know how much time you have before the creditors come and take your home, cars, family, and your life away from you. Ask yourself how much time will you have if your income suddenly stopped either by illness or job loss before your mortgage, Master Card and Visa starts calling. If you have accumulated wealth, you can hold them off forever in some cases.

Passive income is an income received on a regular basis, without working or with little effort required to maintain it. Such as from: stock dividends, bonds, rents, royalties etc. Well let's measure your wealth in time.

FINANCIAL SECURITY AND WEALTH MEASURED IN TIME:

Cash and assets easily turned into cash i.e bonds, stocks etc

Divided by: Monthly expenses minus passive income = Time

If your passive income is greater than your expenses, then you are financially free

Exam:

Tim was just laid off from his accountant job where he was earning an $80,000 yearly salary. He has a family of four. His cash in the bank is $2,000 and his cash equivalent: 401k stock and bonds mutual funds are $11,000. He has no other income. His family monthly expenses are $3,700.

Cash and cash equivalent: $2,000 + $11,000 = $13,000

Divided by his monthly expenses of $3,700 = Time: 3 ½ months.

Tim's wealth will allow him to survive 3 ½ months before he began to lose everything he has worked for.

WORKSHEET

Things to remember	Actions To-Do	Dates

Let's perform the same calculation with passive income of $1,500 from Tim's annuity and his rental home.

Cash and cash equivalent: $2,000 + $11,000 = $13,000

Divided by his monthly expenses of $3,700 minus passive income of $1,500 = $2,200

Now his wealth measured in time changes to: $13,000/$2,200 = 6 months. By having passive income, he can survive a full 6 months before his wealth becomes deficient. Tim's goal is to have all of his expenses paid for by his passive income, then he is considered financially secured.

OK IT'S YOUR TURN TO PERFORM THIS CALCULATION ON YOURSELF:

<u>Cash +   Cash Equivalents</u>
Monthly expenses – Passive income

= Your financial security and wealth measured in time

F*CK YOU EMERGENCY MONEY- IN CASE YOU LOSE YOUR JOB

Keep in mind that you are in a war, a financial war. There will always come a time when out of the blues, un-expectantly, your income stops, either as result of corporate downsizing, you get fired or you just can't take it anymore and you quit your job. For, whatever reasons you will need an emergency fund or attitude money. I call it f*ck you money! Your Emergency Fund should be in a bank that is FDIC (Federal Deposit Insurance Corporation) protected against lost up to $250,000 per bank account. FDIC protects your funds from frauds and failures. A ROTH IRA can serve this purpose only if your money is saved in an FDIC protected account. A side benefit from the ROTH is that interest income is not taxed if you stay invested in the ROTH for 5 years or more. Your ROTH fund representative can give you the latest details. We will review IRA's in the next section. Here, we are only interested in preservation of principal and to make sure you don't lose any of this money in stock market investments

WORKSHEET

Things to remember	Actions To-Do	Dates

You are not interested in risking any of this money for a return on this money. If you use your bank's Money Market fund for the purpose of earning interest just make sure it is FDIC protected. This account is to ensure that if you have an interruption in your income, you will be able to meet your major expenses until you get back to work or your income stream continues. This fund will stop the creditors, banks, and government tax collectors from taking your life that you have worked so hard for away from you. This fund will stop them from taking your home, your cars, cutting off your utilities, and providing food for your family. **You must save to meet emergencies and short-term expenses for at least 3 to 6 months and even more until you feel comfortable.**

You want to cover your basic expenses like your mortgage or rent, cars, utility, food, insurance, any medicine etc. These items should be included in your emergency fund. You really don't need to include your 250 channels premium HBO subscription, your monthly fitness center and your weekly hair dresser, finger and toe nail salon fees into your emergency fund. This fund is for your major living expenses only. By just covering your major expenses will reduce the amount that you must accumulate in this fund. We will be discussing saving for your investment plans later in the following chapters. All savings whether to meet your short term needs and investing to meet your long term financial freedom/retirement needs should be automated. These funds should come automatically out of your payroll check directly into your savings and investment plans. This way you will not be forced to make any decisions about how much to save and where to put it each month. It's all automated and done for you. Review a sample Emergency Account Summary on the next page, You can make it as simple or as robust as you want to. The idea is for you to feel ready in case of an emergency or your income suddenly stops.

WORKSHEET

Things to remember	Actions To-Do	Dates

EMERGENCY EXPENSES	Montly payment	How many months	Total Funds
Mortgage/rent payment	$ 950.00	3	$ 2,850.00
Transportation (gas, tolls repairs etc)	$ 150.00	3	$ 450.00
Utilities	$ 150.00	3	$ 450.00
Auto loans	$ 250.00	3	$ 750.00
Groceries	$ 250.00	2	$ 500.00
Medicine			
Insurance	$ 150.00	2	$ 300.00
Emergency savings account total	$ 1,900.00		$ 5,300.00

Go to APPENDIX SECTION "G" for a blank Emergency Money form. Make as many copies as you need.

GET INTO MONEY MAKING DEBT
AND CREATE WEALTH

This is the secret of the rich. They get into debt that makes them money, they use OPM. So not all debt is bad. There is a saying: **There are two types of people, those who earn interest and those who pay interest**. Which one are you? This is the only question that you must answer when it comes to debt. If you are the type of person that earns interest, then congratulations you are doing just fine. However, if you are the person that only pays interest then you must understand that a full third of your lifetime million dollars will go just to make interest payments. There is only one reason to go into debt good or bad and that is to create more value. Debt in the hands of a financial educated person creates wealth and value for himself and others. The same debt in the hands of a person that has not been trained to use debt ends in their very own destruction, demise and bankruptcy, same debt, just knowledge that makes all the difference.

Your criteria for using debt is to buy assets that creates value, goes up in value, allows you to get a reduction in your taxes meaning you can shelter some of your income from a job from taxes. Keep in mind that what enables you to get into debt good or bad is your good credit rating. Don't use your good credit rating against yourself use it to become wealthy. So let's keep our good credit rating and turn this around and make them pay us interest so we can have more money for life not them. Understand that good credit is the key that unlocks the banks vault. Isn't that what you want, more money?

It is almost impossible to live debt-free, most of us cannot pay cash for our homes, cars or our children's college education, so we must learn to manage our debt, and to understand what negative impact that debt has on our life plans. We all use debt in fact our economy runs off the stuff look at the government they are in $18 trillion of debt. The difference between the rich and the poor and middle class is how they use this debt. Rich people are in debt up to their eye balls but it's good debt or the type of debt that pays them a enough money to pay the debt back plus a profit. The rich buy assets that appreciates over time. This is how they got rich in the first place. I do this with rental homes. I borrow the money to buy the rental homes and the tenants pay all the debt and pay me a return every month.

The poor and middle class use debt as well but the only difference is that they use bad debt or the type of debt that make them pay the lender interest payments in which the debtors get no return. The money to pay the debt back comes out of their future earning thus making then poorer. This is why they feel poorer at the end of the month. The poor and middle class buy things that rapidly depreciates in value. The difference between these two groups is financial knowledge that's it. The difference between the rich and everybody else is financial knowledge.

Ideally, experts say your total monthly long-term debt payments, including your mortgage and credit cards, should not exceed 36% of your gross monthly income. That's one metric mortgage bankers consider when assessing the credit worthiness of a potential borrower. So look at all of those bad debt payments that you are paying every month and say good-bye to them. This is bad debt however, we are going to turn these bad debts into good debt and go straight to investing this money to make you wealthy not them.,.

Constructive good debt: This is good debt that produces some type of value. I remember my principle: *If it helps me reduce my taxes, produce income and can increase my net worth over time then I consider it productive and I will go into the debt.*

Example: Sam was looking to reduce his credit cards debt. He has a credit card with a 19% interest rate. Sam a homeowner was approved for a home equity loan at 5% to pay off and close out these cards. Look, Sam has just reduced his interest rate by 14%! But it gets even better. Sam can also share the cost with the government! Since Sam is in the 25% tax bracket his actual interest rate is only 3.75% not 5%, because 25% of his home equity interest rate is tax deductible. To me this is considered a good use of debt. When you pay off debt it's just like getting a return on your money. In this case, Sam is getting a 19% return on his money by paying off and closing out these fairy cards.

Constructive debt is leverage, meaning you can acquire more with less of your money while using (OPM) other people's money or the banks money. The interest is the cost of the debt so bear that in mind. You should weight the use of debt carefully because it does carry a risk reward scenario. All investment has its downside so there is not a 100% guarantee on any investment they all have risk and rewards. But if you have carefully considered downside to any investment and have accepted the calculated risk then go ahead. You should not make any investments that if it does not turn out profitable, it would cause you to go into insolvency. This is called being over leveraged. If insolvency is the risk, you may want to reconsider the investment or reduce the amount of debt you are using as leverage needed to make the investment.

Example: Debbie a homeowner decided to purchase a rental property for $95,000. She checked the property out and determined that it can provide her monthly rental income of $1,000. She decided to put a down payment of 15% or $14,250 by getting a 5% (3.75% after tax) home equity loan and the bank would carry the note, OPM. The monthly payment for this loan was $575 monthly tax and interest included. Her monthly cash flow is $425 ($1,000 – $575). The cash flow was created from nothing. To me this is good productive debt.

EXAMPLES OF GOOD CONSTRUCTIVE DEBT

College education: It's more favorable to have a professional degree than not because it can better position you in getting jobs that produces enough income to repay the loan. Certain college-educated people with bachelor's degree are being paid on average 66% more than those with only a high school diploma according to The U.S. Department of Education's National Center for Education Statistics (NCES).

Business & Real Estate loans: **Borrow for a business purpose and receive a tax deduction on the interest**. Yes, Uncle Sam will help you pursue the American Dream of real estate and business ownership. Since the main reasons we go into business in the first place is to earn income while our business grows and appreciates over time. Just make sure you have a solid business with solid profits before you acquire any debt, because you want to use the additional profits from acquiring the debt to repay the loan.

Again, these are some example of what I call Productive or good debt. You will have to weigh all the benefits pros and cons when using debt because it can turn around and bite you. Just make sure you are not over leveraged because while leverage is good on the up side it works 100% against you on the downside or when the thing does not work out as planned. So use a little moderation and don't go too far out on a limb.

DESTRUCTIVE DEBT TAKES MORE MONEY FROM YOU THAN IT GIVES!

REMEMBER: There are two types of people, those you earn interest and those who pay interest.

Destructive bad debt: If you have this debt then you are the type of person that pays interest. You should not go into debt to buy stuff that creates zero value and that goes down in value. This is the definition of bad debt. Bad debt does not generate more income for you and cannot increase your net worth over time. Keep in mind that people become poorer if they use debt to buy stuff that goes down in value or depreciates.

SOME EXAMPLES OF BAD DEBT

Credits cards (fairy cards): If you use credit cards and make the minimum payments then interest is being compounded 100% against you. You know how the banks pay you interest on top of interest in your bank account, well with a credit card compound interest is being applied against you.

Example: Say if you have $1,000 in your saving account that pays 5%. In year one you will have $1,050 ($1,000 x 5%). Now, in year two you will have a balance of $1,102.50 ($1,050 x 5%). See how you are being paid interest on top of interest? Now imagine instead of the bank paying you this compound interest you are paying the bank compound interest. Same example just turn it around. Compound interest pointed against us is the reason we become poorer.

In other words you are paying the banks interest on top of interest. Carrying a balance and making minimum payments is probably the single biggest reason that makes people poor. Credit card interest rates are high and you will pay much more that the cost of the original purchase if you carry a balance. However, the average household carries a $15,000 credit card balance and climbing, this means that the poor are getting poorer and the rich banks that has the money to lend is getting richer. Let's **CUT THEM OFF NOW!** Let them go get their fix from somebody else.

Consumable and fads items: Have you noticed that Americans are wearing, carrying, walking and talking all on debt. These fads are: clothes the latest Smart-Phones travel and entertainment etc., this brings them no value after the initial purchase. There is never a good reason to go into debt to make these purchases and carry a balance that you will pay interest on for years to come. Then if you for whatever reason you miss several payments it can ruin your credit rating and of course you will be access a higher interest rate which will cost you more money. Women love sales, but I have literally seen them go broke saving money. Usually when there is a big sale for food or consumables items the savings are eaten up by the interest payments you pay when you use a credit card.

Cars: People are driving debt. Beware of the **minimum payment debt trap.** Yes, cars are needed to earn income in most cases so it meets the first criteria. However, since it loses a big chunk of its value or depreciates when you drive it off the car lot, it just makes since to pay for these cars with cash. However, there are times when you need transportation now. If you just don't have the cash saved up then purchase an inexpensive pre-owned vehicle like I did and pay it off as soon as possible. Then save up cash for your next vehicle. Keep in mind there are tags, license, maintenance, and insurance cost associated with these cars on top of the debt or monthly payments. We all have a problem here in America, the marketers have taught us how to look and only see the minimum payments and not the full cost. Next time you make a purchase ask to see the full cost of the item. Then make your decision. Remember this all has to come from your lifetime million dollars that you are going to earn.

PHASE 2:
CUT YOUR TAXES IN HALF

16TH AMENDMENT - THE POWER TO *"TAKE"* TAX YOUR MONEY

*"Any one may so arrange his affairs that his taxes shall
be as low as possible; he is not bound to choose that pattern
which will best pay the Treasury; there is not even a patriotic
duty to increase one's taxes."*
Judge Learned Hand

THE XVI AMENDMENT to the United States Constitution allows the Congress to levy an income tax without apportioning it among the states or basing it on the United States Census. This amendment exempted income taxes from the constitutional requirements regarding direct taxes, after income taxes on rents, dividends, and interest.

This simply means that Congress has the power to tax (take) income (the money that you earn) from all sources. In other words, the politicians do not have to give an account to you before they take your money. You do not get a vote to determine when and how much taxes they will levy on you. The reason that you are broke is not that you are forced to pay approximately 50% of your income from a job as taxes to the governments, but you do not have the knowledge to reduce your taxes and invest this money to make yourself wealthy. You must become tax efficient if you are going to stop them from taking so much of your money. It's time to educate yourselves and fight back. Like the Judge says: *you do not have a duty to pay any more in taxes than you should.* Let's get to work, let's CUT THEM OFF!

TO BENEFIT FROM THE TAX LAWS, YOU MUST UNDERSTAND THE TAX SYSTEM

The federal income tax system has a simple logic behind it. Most taxpayers see it as a complex mathematical numbers game. They believe that the IRS is out to get them so they become very fearful of the process and this fear prevents them from ever understanding the basic simplicity of the tax system and how this system can benefit them through deductions and credits. This fear of the tax system causes them to pay more in taxes than they should. The truth is that any 5th grader can do the simple math. That's because the tax system is more about words than math, should I file as single or head of household, should I itemize or take the standard deduction, should I take a deduction for my IRA contributions? etc.

Below is a very simplified version of the tax system. Computing one's taxes can be quite complex but understanding the basics can allow you to use the system to benefit you. Here in a nutshell is the essence of the federal tax system:

BASIC FEDERAL INCOME TAX FORMULA

	Gross Income
Less:	Deductions for AGI
Equal:	Adjusted Gross Income (AGI)
Less:	Greater of: 1) Itemized Deductions or 2) Standard Deductions
Less:	Exemption Amount
Equal:	Taxable Income
X	Income Tax Rate
Equal:	Regular Income Tax
Plus:	Other Taxes
Less:	Tax Payments
Less:	Credits
Equal	Tax Due or (Refund)

This is all you need to know. The real issue is not arithmetic. It's what to include as income, what you can deduct from income, and where to invest to avoid reporting income at all?

DEFINITIONS FROM THE IRS INCOME TAX SYSTEM:

Gross Income: Gross income means all income from whatever source derived.

Deductions for AGI: Individual taxpayers has two categories of deductions: 1) deductions for adjusted gross income (AGI) or deductions to arrive at AGI and 2) deductions from AGI. However, deductions from AGI include ordinary and necessary expenses incurred in trade or business, one half of self-employment tax paid, alimony paid, IRA contributions, Medical Saving Accounts, moving expenses, forfeited interest penalty for premature withdrawal of time deposits, capital loss deductions and others.

Adjusted Gross Income (AGI): AGI is an important subtotal that serves as the basis for computing limitations on certain itemized deductions such as medical expenses and charitable contributions, and more. If your AGI is too high that can make you ineligible for certain tax deductions. For instance, the medical expense are only deductible to extent that they exceed 7.5% of AGI, and certain Charitable contributions deductions may not exceed 50% of AGI.

Itemized Deductions: As a rule, personal expenditures are disallowed as deductions in arriving at taxable income. However, Congress has chosen to allow specific personal expenses as itemized deductions. Such expenditures include: mortgage interest, medical expenses, certain taxes paid, charitable contributions and many more. All designed to lower your taxes or get you a bigger refund.

Standard Deductions: The standard deduction which is set by congress is a specific amount of deductible dollars that depends on your filing status. The effect of the standard deduction is to exempt a taxpayer's income up to the specified amount from Federal Income tax liability.

Personal Exemption: The use of exemptions in the tax system is based in part on the idea that a taxpayer with a small amount of income should be exempt from income taxation. An exemption frees a specific amount of income from taxes. A taxpayer who claims an individual as a dependent is allowed to claim an exemption for that dependent. However, the dependent cannot claim a personal exemption on his or her tax returns.

Taxable Income: This is the amount after deductions that are subject to income taxes

Income Tax Rate: The rates are set by Congress and adjusted periodically. At the present, there are seven Federal income tax brackets: 10%, 15%, 25%, 28%, 33%, 35%, and 39.6%. The amount of tax you owe depends on your income level and filing status.

Other taxes: These are other taxes not captured in other areas of the regular tax calculations such as: self-employment taxes, unreported social security and medical taxes, additional taxes on IRAs or other retirement plans, repayment of first time homebuyer credits and others.

Payments: This represents tax payments previously made by the filers: Federal income tax withheld from (W2) and 1099 estimated tax payments, earned income credits, taxes paid with extensions, additional child care credits and more.

Tax credits: Federal law often serves other purposes besides raising money for the government. The citizens social and economic considerations are found throughout the tax laws. To provide for these considerations, the government provides tax credits which is a dollar for dollar reduction to your tax bill.

Tax due or refund: Underpayment or overpayment of your taxes.

THE GOVERNMENT PAYS YOU - WHEN YOU BUY A HOME AND START A RETIREMENT PLAN

Taxes are only an enemy to the people that do not take the time to understand some basic rules. Keep in mind that it is important to familiarize yourself with these basic rules because you will pay a third to one half of all the money that you earn in taxes. So, understanding basic tax rules can work as an asset to you. How you ask? The average person largest expenses is their home purchases and saving for their retirement. THE GOVERNMENT PAYS YOU MONEY FOR BOTH EXPENSES. You see it is the government that allows you to take a deduction and pay less taxes so you can have more money to pay your mortgage, not the bank. This means that the government PAYS you when you purchase your home. The GOVERNMENT ALSO PAYS YOU BY subsidizing your 401k, IRAs and other retirement plans by allowing you to pay less in taxes so you can have more money to invest for your future. The trick with taxes is to make investments where the tax rules favors you not them. You do this by becoming knowledgeable about the tax laws and planning. If you do not take the time to consider basic tax reduction strategies, well then just send a third to one half of your lifetime earnings to Washington DC.

WORKSHEET

Things to remember | **Actions To-Do** | **Dates**

Example: David wanted to start saving for his retirement using a 401k. As one of his plan selection David chose to use the Stable Value Dollar fund because his money would not fluctuate with the ups and downs like the stock market and there would be no risk of losing his money. David was in the 25% tax bracket. For simplicity, he invested $10,000 in his retirement. Since he was in the 25% tax bracket, he would receive a $10,000 reduction in his taxable income, which is worth $2,500 ($10,000 x 25%). So, good old Uncle Sam PAID him $2,500. His returns on a simple money market mutual fund was 25% not the 1% that is advertised. Now can you tell me where you can get a 25% return without taking any risk of principal. You see understanding basic tax rules can be an asset to you.

THE TAX RULES BENEFIT THE INVESTOR/ PRODUCER NOT THE CONSUMER

*People who complain about the tax system fall
into two categories ---men and women.*
Barry Steiner

The first rule in understanding how to create wealth using the tax laws are to understand that tax laws benefits the investor producer not the working wage earner. Most wealthy people are investors. So, the tax laws benefit wealthy people.

Look below I have provided an income tax table to prove my point. To be an investor/producer means that you are taxed differently or less than the wage earner. See below the tax rates paid on ordinary income and investor's income *(dividends and long term capital gains)*.

WORKSHEET

Things to remember   **Actions To-Do**   **Dates**

2016 Federal Income Tax Brackets				
Tax rates on earned and ordinary income	SINGLE			Tax rates on qualified dividends and long term capital gains
	start	stop		
10%	$0	$9,275		0%
15%	$9,275	$37,650		0%
25%	$37,650	$91,150		15%
28%	$91,150	$190,150		15%
33%	$190,150	$413,350		15%
35%	$413,350	$415,050		15%
39.60%	$415,050			20%
	Married filing jointly/Widower			
	start	stop		
10%	$0	$18,550		0%
15%	$18,550	$75,300		0%
25%	$75,300	$151,900		15%
28%	$151,900	$231,450		15%
33%	$231,450	$413,350		15%
35%	$413,350	$466,950		15%
39.60%	$466,950			20%

Source: IRS.

Notice above there are 7 tax brackets for the ordinary or earned income that you receive from a job. They range from 10% to 39.6%. However, notice that if you received your income from investments then there are only 3 tax brackets, 0% to 20%. Now which set of taxes would you like to pay? Can you see how the rich get richer? It's because they do not work for their income, they receive income from their investments. The tax law favors the investor not the hard-working wage earner.

THIS IS HOW THE IRS TAX YOU

Let me explain how taxes are really paid through the progressive tax system. From just looking at the ordinary income tax brackets it would appear that if a person enters a particular tax bracket then all of his income is taxed at that rate. Say, if a single person earned $50,000 annually then according to the table above they would be in the 25% tax bracket and all of their income is taxed at that rate. This is misleading because America uses a progressive tax system. The tax system is designed to ensure that the people that earns the least wages pays a lower tax margin and the people earns the most in wages pays the higher margins.

Example: If a single person earns $100,000 from his job looking at the tables it looks like he would be paying all his income at the 28% tax rate or $28,000. This does not take into consideration deductions, exemptions, and credits. This is not true due to our progressive tax system his actual tax due is calculated from the table as such:

- 10% on the first $9.275 of earned income,
- 15% for the portion up to $37,650,
- 25% for the portion up to $91,150,
- and 28% for the remainder.

Total tax due without exemptions, deductions and credits considered is: $21,037 not $28,000.

Now let's compare taxes rates for qualified dividends and long term capital gains vs ordinary income

Example: If a single person earned $50,000 from his job wages he would have to pay $5,684 in federal taxes. If this same single person received the same $50,000 from his investments only as qualified dividends he would only owe just $300 in federal taxes. Wow what a difference! Again, this is how the wealthy stay wealthy. They simply do not work for a living they receive income from their investments.

PLAN TO PAY LESS TAXES

"I expect to spend the rest of my life in the future,
so I want to be reasonably sure what kind of future it's going to be.
That's my reason for planning."
C. Kettering

The only reason to decide and make a Tax Plan is to pay the least amount of taxes possible. Tax planning allows you to control the amount of taxes that you pay. Judge Learned Hand's quote underscores your responsibility he said   *"Any one may so arrange his affairs that his taxes shall be as low as possible"*. The Judge stated the each of us has a patriotic duty to pay as little taxes as legally possible. Any savings from taxes can be used for your financial freedom not the taxing politicians. So why is taxes the largest expense each of us will ever have? Simply because we fail to adhere to this Judge. We simply do not plan and therefore we pay the maximum taxes possible. As a CPA, I have had the pleasure of preparing thousands of tax returns over my lifetime. And the battle cry that I always here is that they pay too much in taxes. And they are correct. I beg them to understand some simple principles of reducing their taxes by planning. The simplest and most basic way to reduce your taxes is found in these three areas. 1) Reduce your taxable income 2) Increase allowable deductions and 3) Take all credits available to you. That's it.

The IRS nor your tax preparer is responsible to get you to walk into your tax preparer's office and make a plan. Planning starts January 1st not April 15th. Every January 1st meet with your Tax Professional and ask them how can you pay less taxes this year that you did last year? Your goal is to create more money to spend and invest by reducing your taxes. You are simply trying to get some of your money back from the government to create wealth for yourself.

THREE STRATEGIES TO CUT YOUR TAXES IN HALF

STRATEGY #1   REDUCE TAXABLE INCOME
STRATEGY #2   INCREASE DEDUCTIONS
STRATEGY #3   USE TAX CREDITS

That's it. This is what all the fuss is all about. Now there are many techniques and variations for each of these strategies but for now we will focus on the majors, the biggest bang for your buck!. Keep it simple.

Who Should File an Income Tax Return:
According to the IRS website, even if you don't have to file, you should file a tax return to see if you can get money back. For example, you should file if one of the following applies:

- *You had income tax withheld from your pay.*
- *You made estimated tax payments for the year or had any of your overpayment for last year applied to this year's estimated tax.*
- *You qualify for the earned income credit. See Pub. 596, Earned Income Credit (EIC), for more information.*

- *You qualify for the additional child tax credit. See the instructions for the tax form you file (Form 1040 or 1040A) for more information.*
- *You qualify for the refundable American opportunity education credit. See Form 8863, Education Credits.*
- *You qualify for the health coverage tax credit. For information on this credit, see Form 8885.*
- *You qualify for the credit for federal tax on fuels. See Form 4136, Credit for Federal Tax Paid on Fuels.*

USING THE WRONG TAX FORMS WILL COST YOU MONEY

The IRS will accept any way that you want to file your taxes as long as you don't underpay them. There are several ways to file your taxes but only one way that will get you the biggest refund. If you want to ensure that you take all tax deductions and credits that you are legally entitled to then you need to know your tax forms. Yes, your tax forms will uncover all of those hidden tax deductions that is available to you. Let's review below:

The 1040 is the only income tax form that is updated yearly by the IRS themselves that will allow you to deduct every available tax deduction available to you.

The 1040A is designed to limit the deductions that you may be entitled to. So as a result, your refund may be smaller.

The 1040EZ form does not allow any deductions or adjustments to your taxable income. In other words: ***if you are using this form you are guaranteeing yourself that you will pay the highest tax possible no matter how much of a tax refund that you get back.***

These are all talking points that you need to discuss with your tax professional. The leading tax software like Turbo Tax is a do it yourself process. It will guide you to use the correct tax forms that will allow you to get the biggest allowable deductions thereby the biggest refunds.

STRATEGY #1
REDUCE YOUR TAXABLE INCOME

Reducing your income starts with understanding what constitutes income as it relates to taxes. You will find throughout this section that not all income is taxable.

Gross income

According to the IRS gross income is defined to be all income from whatever source derived, including (but not limited to) the following items: **(1)** Compensation for services, including fees, commissions, fringe benefits, and similar items; **(2)** Gross income derived from business; **(3)** Gains derived from dealings in property; **(4)** Interest; **(5)** Rents; **(6)** Royalties; **(7)** Dividends; **(8)** Alimony and separate maintenance payments; **(9)** Annuities; **(10)** Income from life insurance and endowment contracts; **(11)** Pensions; **(12)** Income from discharge of indebtedness; **(13)** Distributive share of partnership gross income; **(14)** Income in respect of a decedent; and **(15)** Income from an interest in an estate or trust.

The good news is that not all income is subject to income taxes. See a full list below:

Non-Taxable Income

This is simply income that is exempt from taxes by the IRS. Wouldn't it be nice to have lots of nontaxable income? This means every dollar earned is going into your pocket to make you wealthy and you don't have to share it with the government. Nontaxable income includes all of receipts that taxpayers mistakenly report to the IRS. Make sure you are not lining the government's politicians pockets with taxes on income you don't have to report. You can go to IRS Publication 525, Taxable, and Nontaxable Income to find more examples of nontaxable income. Below is just a small sample:

List of Non-Taxable Income

Federal income tax refunds, State income tax refunds (if you did not itemize deductions that year), Loans, Retirement plans (IRA, 401k's etc.) rollovers, Life Insurance (death benefits) proceeds, Capital Gains on sale of your home (up to $500,000 for married couples), Divorce settlements property, Gift and inheritances, Municipal bond interest (ATM may apply), Child support payments, Lawsuit settlements from personal injuries, Certain disability income, Scholarships used for school purposes, Health savings accounts (HSA), Workers' Compensation, and certain Interest on qualified savings bonds.

TO PAY LESS TAXES - LOWER YOUR AGI (ADJUSTED GROSS INCOME)

Your AGI is the most important number on your tax return because it will not only determine the size of your refund and tax bill, but it will also determine the maximum amount of deductions and credits that is available to you. Its called line 37 if you file a 1040 tax return. This one line will determine penalties, surtaxes and most importantly, phase outs of tax deductions. The tax code is filled with assaults on your AGI. So, it is in the best interest of the taxpayer to develop a plan to lower their AGI as much as possible.

Your AGI is on the first page of your tax returns. It is calculated by adding the total amount of your income that is subject to taxes by the IRS and reducing that number by allowable deductions which decrease your AGI and your tax bill. Gross income includes such items as wages from your job, self-employment income, alimony receipts, as well as interest earned from your bank account just to name a few. Once you get your total income then you can reduce this number by deductions that you are allowed to take such as self-employment expenses, Health Saving Accounts (HSA), student loan interest payments and IRAs except a ROTH, just to mention a few. This amount equal your taxable net income or AGI.

Example: Tom has a gross income from his job of $80,000 for the tax year 2016. His allowable deductions from his 401k and small business losses reduces his AGI to be only $55,000. Tom also has interest payments from his college student loan of $2,500. For the 2016 tax year, you can deduct up to $2,500 in student loan interest if your modified AGI is $65,000 or less. Tom can further reduce his taxable income by the full $2,500 because his AGI is less than the IRS limitation of $65,000. If his AGI would have remained at $80,000 he would have not been eligible to qualify for this deduction. So, for tax purposes your AGI is more important than your gross income. Banks also review your AGI in determining mortgages and other loans that you can qualify for. So, if you want to pay less taxes you must focus and find ways to reduce your AGI.

ITEMS THAT REDUCES YOUR AGI INCLUDES:

Self-employment business expenses, Half of self-employment taxes, Self-Employment retirement accounts (SEP and SIMPLE IRAs, 401k qualified plans), Employment 401ks retirement plans, Rental activity expenses, Individual Retirement Accounts (IRAs), Health savings account deductions, Certain moving expenses, Alimony payments,

College tuition fees, and student loan interest with limitations, Capital losses on investments etc. just to name a few.

STRATEGY #2:
REDUCE YOUR TAXES WITH THE BIG 7 DEDUCTIONS

1. PERSONAL EXEMPTIONS

Congress created deductible exemptions so that you and your dependents are exempt from personally being taxed. Thereby allowing you to get payment in a refund from the government. Tax exemptions are not just for you. The government exempts certain organizations and business from being taxed such as charities, public education, and religious organizations. They are exempt completely from taxes because the government feels that these organizations serve the public. These exemptions reduce taxable income the same as any deduction but with much less restrictions. The only restriction is that no one else can claim you as a dependent at the same time. Say if you are married, both you and your wife are exempt from taxation. This exemption increases ever year with inflation. For 2016, each exemption is worth $4,050, however, certain personal exemption phase-outs occurs for high income earners so if you get confused discuss with a tax professional.

Example: Tom and Sue are married and have two small children, their total exemption deductions for the year 2016 is $16,200 ($4,050 x 4).

GET A TAX-FREE RAISE IN YOUR NEXT PAYCHECK

You can increase your take-home pay by increasing the number of exemptions called allowances that you claim on your Form W-4, Employee's Withholding Allowance Certificate at your job. This form is required by your employer so they can withhold the correct amount of federal taxes from your paycheck. Most employees claim too few allowances thus causing them to get a big tax refund. But the truth is that the refund is no more than a return of your own money. The IRS did not give you anything. By claiming too few allowances than you are eligible for means that you just gave the IRS an interest free loan. When you file your taxes, and discover that you are due a refund the IRS will return your money to you later without paying you any interest. Now try borrowing from or owing the IRS and see what you will pay, interest on top of interest on top of penalties until you pay what you owe. Therefore, you should complete a new Form W-4 each year as changes in your personal or other financial events occurs.

WORKSHEET

Things to remember | **Actions To-Do** | **Dates**

As you know when you file your taxes on April 15th you must report the correct amount of exemptions. So be careful because claiming to few allowances than you are entitled means that you will give the IRS an interest free loan and your take home pay will be smaller. However, claiming too many allowances means that your employer may not withhold enough taxes from your paycheck and this can result in penalties. The good news is that allowances does not only apply to personal and dependents exemptions but they can also be taken for other expenses like charitable contributions, taxes paid, and one of the biggest: mortgage interest deductions, and many more.

Example: Bob and Mary Smith married with two children are in the 25% tax bracket and they receive a tax refund every year. They decided that they want to get a tax-free pay raise now instead of sending this interest free loan to the IRS every year. To get this increase in pay now they must determine how many allowances to claim on their W-4. Each allowance is worth $4,050 for the year 2016. So, with these numbers let's do the simple math to get more money in the Smiths pay check now:

Step 1: Calculate how much money a deduction or an allowance is worth:

Allowance $4,050 x .25 = $1,012.50. So, to keep this simple every allowance that you claim means that you are entitled to receive a $1,012.50 increase in your pay check for the year.

Step 2: Determine your yearly pay check increase by adding up all of your allowances:

		Deduction		Tax	Increase
4 Dependents:	$4,050 x 4 =	$16,200	x	.25 =	$4,050
Home mortgage interest:		$8,500	x	.25 =	$2,125
Total		$25,300			**$6,175**

Instead of using the Smith's paycheck increase of **$6,175** calculation above, you can just get a copy of your last year actual refund, use your refund number, and skip this step.

Say if you had a $2,000 refund then just use your number where you see the Smith's $6,125 number.

Step 3: Translate this refund into the correct amount of allowances to claim on your W-4 so you can get your refund starting in your next paycheck.

Divide the refund of $6,175 / $1,012.50 = 6 exemptions.

WORKSHEET

Things to remember   **Actions To-Do**   **Dates**

So tomorrow, Tom will go to his employer and increase his W-4 allowance to 6. I like a little cushion myself so I will use 4 instead of 6. This is just personal. **Remember the more allowances that you claim, the less your employer will withhold from your paycheck to pay your taxes, the bigger your paycheck. This is the good side. The bad side is that if your employer does not withhold enough taxes for you, you may have to pay a penalty when you file your yearly taxes. So, be careful and seek some help from your tax professional if you get confused. You do not want to owe the IRS any money because they can charge you interest and penalties.**

Step 4: Calculate the increase on the Smith next month paycheck:

Divide the refund $6,175 by 12 months = $515 extra money tax free each month! Put this in your pocket, pay down debt, invest it, or go on a mini vacation. The choice is yours. The point is that you get to use this extra money now instead of sending it to Washington DC interest free then waiting for a refund.

Ok now that you have worked through this example. Take a moment and calculate how much you can increase your next paycheck. Review the example above. Check with your tax professional for help if you need it.

2. STANDARD DEDUCTION VS. ITEMIZED DEDUCTION STANDARD DEDUCTIONS:

The standard deduction is an amount of money that you are allowed to reduce your taxable income whether you have any other deductions or not. For the tax year 2016, you can reduce your taxable income by these amounts.

- $6,300 deduction if you are single
- $12,600 deduction if you are married and filing jointly
- $6,300 deduction if you are married and filing separately
- $9,300 deduction if you are a head of household.

Example: Tom and Sue are married and will file their 2016 income taxes jointly. They have a combined income of $90,000. Their standard deduction is $12,600. This will allow them to reduce their taxable income to $77,400 ($90,000 – $12,600). They are in the 30% tax bracket. Their income tax saving from the standard deduction is $$3,780 ($12,600 x 30%).

Additional Standard Deduction: For taxpayers who are 65 or older and/or blind, is allowed to receive even larger standard deduction amounts. The age and the visually impaired for each spouse is counted separately. This additional deduction each is worth $1,250 per individual. If you are a single taxpayer you can get and additional $1,550 deduction.

ITEMIZED DEDUCTIONS:

The IRS has allowed you even more ways to reduce your taxable income called *"Itemized deductions"*. Using the Standard Deductions can place a limit on your deductions. But if you have more deductible items such as: real estate taxes, mortgage interest payments, charitable deductions etc., as listed on the tax form Schedule A, then you can get even a bigger deduction. It's best to compare both the standard deductions and the itemize deductions to see which will give you the biggest deductions.

Example: Tom and Sue are married in the 30% tax bracket, their savings from the standard deduction was $3,780 ($12,600 x 30%). They had $18,000 worth of qualified deductions from items such as: mortgage interest payments, real estate taxes, state taxes, and charitable contributions etc. they need to use the "Schedule A" form to claim their deductions. Instead of claiming a standard deduction of $3,780, by using the "Itemized Deductions", they can claim a bigger deduction of $5,400 ($18,000 x .30). The lesson here is to make sure you are using the correct tax forms to get the biggest deduction.

Final Note: Keep in mind that the law does not allow you to use both the standard and itemized deductions at the same time. However, you are allowed to choose which one that will give you the biggest tax deduction. This will allow you to reduce your taxable income to its lowest possible level and get you the biggest tax refund. You will pay less taxes which is your only goal here. Remember the Judge quotes; *"Any one may so arrange his affairs that his taxes shall be as low as possible"*. The Judge stated the each of us has a patriotic duty to pay as little taxes as legally possible.

When you combine the exemptions and deductions together most Americans pay little federal taxes.

Example: Jerry and Cindy are married and have two children. Their exemptions are $16,200 (4 x $4,050). Since they are married filing jointly they chose the standard deductions of $12,600. When they combined these two deductions they get a full $28,800 of deductions to reduce their taxable income. They pay less taxes.

3. CONTRIBUTE TO A 401K/IRA RETIREMENT PLAN

For most of us working Americans, contributions to these retirement plans offer us the biggest tax deductions available as well as the ability to maximize our saving and investing for our retirement. ***Remember you are not going to get a pension from your employer. All you get is all you save!*** Retirement plans such as 401k, 403b etc. as well as IRAs, except Roth IRAs, have been created to replace employer provided pension plans. These plans allow tax payers to save the maximum amount of money for their retirement and receive the biggest tax deductions at the same time. As you know big tax deductions lowers your AGI and that can result in the biggest tax refund. Keep in mind that the law does not allow you to receive a tax deduction for both a 401k and a IRA at the same time. However, per eligibility you can take a deduction for contributions made to your non-working spouse IRA. See IRS Pub 590-A or discuss with a IRA provider.

Pay less taxes and make yourself wealthy with retirement plans
A dollar saved is a dollar earned. Well in tax saving terms a tax-free dollar could equal a million dollars earned. You have probably heard this before but it's worth repeating: If you take $1.00 and double it, **tax-free** for 20 days, it will be worth $1,048,576. The rich stays rich because they pay less taxes. Take the same $1.00, now let the IRS tax it every year at a 30% tax rate and it will be worth ONLY $40,640. This is why the poor and middle class stay the poor and middle class. Look here again! **By letting the IRS tax (take) your dollars, YOU HAVE LOST A COOL ONE MILLION DOLLARS!** Now do you believe that reducing your tax burden is important? Well I hope so.

Tax free compounding is called the most silent perpetual wealth building strategy ever created. That's it! Tax free earnings on top of tax free earnings. This means that if your tax free investments yields you a return of 10%, then the principal you invested received 10% and the 10% interest that you earned receives 10% and so it goes forever. Combine this with a tax-free or tax deferred vehicle like your 401k, or real estate investments and you got yourself a land slide a real money machine. It's like an automated machine, once you start the money machine it does the rest all by itself.   If you are in the 28% tax bracket guess what? Ever buck you get to keep is just like getting a 28% return on your money! Now try getting that at your local bank. Compounding in a tax free or deferred environment makes you wealthy. The rich know this and now so do you.

See the table below for allowable contributions and tax deductible limits for 2016:

2016 RETIREMENT PLANS		
Retirement plans tax deferred	Contribution and tax deductible limits	Additional tax savings contributions and deductions for ages 50 and older-catchup
401(k), 403(b) and 457	$18,000	$6,000
SIMPLE IRA	$12,500	$3,000
Self employed-QRP/Keogh and SEP-IRA	20% of net self-employment income (or 25% of compensation) up to $53,000	None
Individual 401(k)	20% of net self-employment income (or 25% of compensation) plus $18,000, up to $53,000	$6,000
Traditional IRA	$5,500	$1,000

IRS source

An employer sponsored 401k has the largest tax deductions of all the employee retirement saving plans. The good news is that these 401k plans are readily available to most earners in America. Per the table above, the IRS will allow you to reduce your taxable income by $18,000, plus an additional $6,000 catch-up contribution for a total of $24,000 if you are over 50 for 401k's retirement plans. *You do not have to worry about claiming this amount as a tax deduction when you file your returns because it's excluded from your taxable income and reported to the IRS as you make contributions through payroll deductions.* If you contributed $10,000 to your 401k and your salary is $60,000, only $50.000 will be reported to the IRS as taxable income.

Example: Tom earned $80,000 without contributing to a 401k. This puts him in the 30% tax bracket. For simplicity, he would have to pay $24,000 in taxes. If Tom contributed $15,000 to his 401k, his taxable income or AGI is now $65,000 reducing his tax bracket to 20%. So now his tax liability would be only $13,000, saving him $11,000 in taxes. And his full $15,000 will be earning tax deferred profits for his retirement future until he must began making withdrawals at age 70 and ½ years old.

The above calculation does not apply to Roth 401k contributions because Roth contributions do not reduce taxable income or AGI since they are made using after tax dollars. In the example above, if Tom made his contribution to a Roth 401k he would not be allowed to reduce his taxable income to $65,000 and would lose the $13,000 savings. The danger here is by not reducing his AGI, his high income can also disqualify him from taking certain other deductions and credits that may have been available to him had he made a plan to reduce his AGI.

4. MORTGAGE INTEREST DEDUCTION

The American dream home ownership. However as patriotic and apple pie this may seem it comes with a cost. But to offset the cost and make home ownership more available and attractive to the average, Congress through the IRS has agreed to pay you or subsidize the cost with you by reducing your tax bill. Since you are either going to pay rent that does not reduce your tax bill or buy a home which will allow you to reduce your tax bill, then you might as well buy a home and payless taxes in the process. In fact, for most people this will be the biggest tax break that they will receive. Since the cost of buying a home is high there is a very good chance that you'll need to borrow the money for the mortgage loan. To help you with the purchase of your new home. The IRS rules allows you to deduct the mortgage interest (not the principal) of your mortgage for your primary residence or a second home. However, the IRS limited the home mortgage deduction to $1.1 million on your primary home, second home and vacation homes.

Example: The Smiths and the Thompsons are two families with the same incomes of $80,000 and both are in the 30% income tax bracket. The Smiths buys their home and pays $1,000 in interest payments each month, or $12,000 annually. The Thompsons did not purchase a home and decided to pay $1,000 a month to rent a single residence. For simplicity, because the Smiths owns their home they can deduct $12,000 from their taxable income using Schedule A, and reduce their taxable income to $62,000. The Thompsons has no deductions and are taxed on the full $80,000 of income. The Smiths saved about $3,600 on taxes. The Thompsons has no deductions and are forced to pay more in taxes.

You can only take this deduction if you itemize your deductions on tax form Schedule A. You can deduct the interest you pay on your primary resident, a second home, a home equity line of credit and a home equity loan. There are also more deductions that are available to you for home ownership: You can also pay less taxes by deducting: Mortgage points, Real estate property taxes, PMI tax deductions and possibly receive a mortgage tax credit. So, make sure you discuss deductions with your tax professional.

5. Rental Property $25,000 Tax Deduction

Before you sell your home, turn it into rental property or buy a property for rental "passive" income and receive as a non-real estate professional up to $25,000 as a tax deduction from other non-rental income. This means you can deduct up to $25,000 of rental losses from your other income, such as wages, salary, and investment income such as dividends, and interest and thus reduce your taxes. Also, a rental home can be a trailer home or even a boathouse on the water and it can be in other states or other countries for that matter, the expenses are all tax deductible. If it's considered a home where you can cook, eat, sleep, and go to the bathroom it can qualify as a rental home.

Even better for those that can qualify as a real estate professional, you can deduct all your rental losses from your non-rental income. So, there are no limits like the $25,000 limit rule. This can be a huge benefit to you and save you a tremendous amount in income taxes every year. Talk to your tax professional or grab a copy of the IRS Pub 925 Passive Activity and At Risk Rules.

The general rule is that passive losses can only be offset by passive income. Passive income is income received on a regular basis from an activity that only requires a small or minimal effort from you to maintain it. There is an exception to this passive rule: **If you actively participate in the operation of the property and your AGI (adjusted gross income) is under $100,000, you can deduct up to $25,000 of passive losses against other income and thus reduce your total tax bill.** This means that you can reduce the taxable income from your job by $25,000 if you qualify. Another benefit of rental income is that you do not pay Social Security and Medicare taxes which can save you 15% on your passive rental income. Therefore, taxes are reduced on passive or rental income.

If a taxpayer actively participates in management decisions i.e. new tenant approval, lease terms, scheduling repairs and capital expenditures etc. for rental properties.

He has met the criteria of actively participation in the real estate leasing activity. In addition, the taxpayer must have at least a 10% interest in the rental activity and if married file a joint tax return for the maximum allowable deduction.

Example: John and Susan Jones filed a joint tax return with an Adjusted Gross Income of $95,000. Susan had a single-family home before the marriage but decided to rent her home rather than sell it. The rental property produced a rental loss for the year of $15,500. The Jones actively participated and managed the rental home. Since the Jones $15,500 loss is below the $25,000 limit and their wages of $95,000 Adjusted Gross Income is below the $100,000 phase-out threshold limit, their entire rental loss is deductible against their non-rental income. Any losses above the $25,000 maximum allowable deduction can be carried forward to later years to offset any income.

Deduction Limits: The IRS has placed phase out limits on the maximum amount of income to qualify for the $25,000 deductions. **The $25,000 deduction starts to phase out between $100,000 and $150,000. However, losses can be carried forward to future years when income can offset losses or until you dispose of the property**. This means that If your Adjusted Gross Income exceeds $100,000 or $50,000 for married filing separately, the $25,000 maximum deduction amount or $12,500 if married filing separately is reduced by .50 of each dollar over $100,000.

Example: John and Susan Jones married filing jointly AGI was $120,000. Therefore, the maximum $25,000 deduction amount is reduced by $10,000 (.50 x $20,000 = $10,000) leaving only $15,000 of their rental losses available to deduct. Since John and Sue had losses of $27,000, this $12,000 loss ($15,000 - $27,000) is carried forward to future years and allowed as a deduction against income. This $12,000 loss can also reduce any gains on the sale of the rental property. Also, if at any time your income falls below the $100,000 phase out limits, you can claim all losses. This will include all future carry over losses as well.

RENTAL HOME EXPENSE TAX WRITE OFFS

All rental expenses just like a business expenses must be ordinary and necessary for the operation of the rental business and are tax deductible. So, make sure that you operate your rental properties just like any other business. Therefore, saving all receipts and other documentations are very important. You will use the IRS tax form

Schedule E to report income and expenses for maintaining your rental properties Below are some of the most common deductible allowed:

- Advertising
- Cleaning and maintenance
- Commissions paid to rental agents
- Home owner association/condo fees
- Home/Landlord Insurance premiums
- Legal fees
- Mortgage interest
- Real Estate Property Taxes
- Utilities
- Vehicle expenses
- Mileage
- Repairs
- Rental related travel
- Depreciation
- Property Management fees
- Pest control
- Professional fees
- Rental of equipment fees
- Rents you paid to others for business purposes
- Supplies
- Landscape fees

To determine your maximum deductible loss use Form 8582: Passive Activity Loss Limitations, or talk with your tax professional.

There is also a 1031 like kind exchange where you can avoid or defer paying taxes on the exchange of your property, again talk to your tax professional for the latest updates.

HOMEOWNERS $500,000 TAX FREE INCOME

If you decide to sell your primary residence, you can make up to $250,000 in profits if you're a single owner, and $500,000 if you're married, and not owe any capital gains taxes on the sale.

This is called the home sale exclusion, you must meet the IRS rules and that is the home must be your primary resident you must live in your home two of the five years before you sell it.

Your home is still one of your biggest tax shelters. You start saving on taxes and building wealth the moment you buy your home and it continues until you decide to sell it. Creating tax sheltered income cannot be easier because you are also allowed to deduct from your taxable income: Mortgage interest, all points paid to get your loan, property tax payments, and applicable interest on home equity loans. These home tax shelters are not just a onetime thing they apply to all of your personal residences that you may own throughout your lifetime as long as you haven't claimed the exclusion on another home in the last two years. However, certain tax laws may change but you get the picture, just make sure you satisfy the IRS requirements, any tax professional can assist you or review pub 523. Want to create wealth through sweat equity? Then buy yourself a fixer-upper. As long as the house is your principal residence you can fix it up while you are meeting your two-year IRS requirements then sell it at a profit.

6. CHARITABLE DONATIONS

According to the IRS you may deduct charitable contributions of money or property made to qualified organizations if you itemize your deductions. Generally, you can deduct up to 50 percent of your adjusted gross income (AGI), but 20 percent and 30 percent limitations apply in some cases.

THE BIG THREE TAX DEDUCTIONS
FOR CHARITY DONATIONS:

1. **Cash donated:** This is the easiest way to make a charitable donation to your favorite charity and practically take a full tax deduction for giving cash. You can simply donate cash or write a check. You are allowed a 50% deduction to your AGI and the charity benefits greatly. Keep in mind that the IRS does not allow you to claim any value that you receive from your donation as a tax deduction. Say if you donate cash of $200 but you received a ticket to a golf tournament worth $25, then you are only allowed to claim $175 as a charitable tax deduction.

2. **Items donated:** Any items, clothing, furniture, appliances, or vehicles are all items that you can donate to your charity and receive a tax deduction.

The IRS does not allow a deduction for items that are old junk or clothes that are not wearable, torn or worn-out. I find that it's best to keep proof of the condition of your donations in pictures or other verifiable documents. If your donations are valued up to $250, the IRS will require a receipt from your charity if possible. If the value of your donations rise to over $500 you will need a receipt from the charity that will verify their name, location, and value of your donations as well as a Form 8283 Noncash Contributions to be filed with your tax returns. If the value of your contributions rise to $5,000 you will need the adjusted basis of the items and any donations over $5,000 requires a written appraisal from a qualified appraiser. Your Tax preparer can assist you in collecting this additional information that is needed to claim these deductions. However, make sure that you get the required documents when you donate these items so the IRS cannot disallow these deductions. Remember the burden of proof is on you.

3. **Expense donated:** You are not allowed a deduction for your hours or time worked and volunteered. However, the IRS does allow you to deduct certain expenses such as mileage, travel expenses and materials purchase for the use in the charity or charitable events. The key here is that you keep detail records of your time, mileage and receipts for materials purchased.

BIG TAX DEDUCTIONS FOR APPRECIATED STOCKS, BONDS AND OTHER SECURITIES DONATED

Donating assets that you have held for more than a year such as stocks, bonds, mutual funds, or other securities is one of the greatest tax reducing methods to give because of two reasons; 1) you can deduct the full increased value of these types of assets to reduce your taxes up to a full 30% of your AGI-Adjusted Gross Income. 2) You avoid paying additional taxes for the long-term capital gains or the increased value of the stocks if you sell the securities. These are both huge tax savings to you with the greatest impact of giving under the tax law.

Example: Tom a plumber has taxable earnings of $70,000. He routinely gives 10% of his income to his church. Tom was informed by his Tax preparer that he can increase his donations and save taxes by donating the long-term assets in his stock mutual fund. Tom invested $4,000 into a stock mutual fund 5 years ago, his investment has increased in value or appreciated to $7,500. If Tom donates the mutual fund to his church, he is allowed to deduct the full appreciated value of the fund and receive a tax deduction of $7,500. He can also avoid paying long term capital gain taxes on the $3,500 gains which saves him $525.

7. HEALTH SAVING ACCOUNTS

To help with your health care expenses the IRS allows you to save and make tax deferred contributions to an HSA - Health Savings Account. This account functions like a IRA, Roth, and a 401k, all combined into one account because the contributions with limits are 100 % tax deductible and the withdrawal are 100% tax free for qualified medical expenses like routine out of pocket medical expenses, dental expenses as well as vision care medical expenses. These accounts have 4 major benefits that may be worth a closer look: 1). Tax deductible contributions 2). Your accumulations grow tax free over the years. 3) You can take withdrawals tax free for your qualified medical expenses. 4) There is no time limitation on taking withdrawals so you can defer indefinitely without any penalties. This is a great way to save for medical expenses for your retirement years.

A side note is that an HSA cannot be used to pay premiums. These accounts can only be used with High Deductible Health Plans (HDHP). Make sure to read the plans because the plans must be MEC or Minimal Essential Coverage plans and not all HDHP are compatible. If you are employed review this with your Benefits Coordinator or otherwise, discuss this with your health care provider before you enroll in the plans.

HOW IT WORKS:

You must decide how much to save and contribute to the HSA for the plan year 2016. For individuals, your maximum contribution is $3,350 and for families it's $6,750. Also, if you are age 55 or older you are allowed and additional $1,000. This brings your total annual contributions for individuals to $4,350 and for families it's $7,750. These contributions are 100% tax deductible to you. See the example below:

YOUR ESTIMATED TAX SAVINGS			
WITHOUT Health Savings Account		WITH Health Savings Account	
Gross Annual Pay	$60,000	Gross Annual Pay	$60,000
Estimated Taxes (30%)	($18,000)	Annual Contribution to H-S-A to be used for healthcare expenses	($6,750)
Net Annual Pay	42,000	Adjusted Gross Pay	$53,250
Estimated Annual Healthcare Expenses	($6,750)	Estimated Taxes (30%)	($15,975)
Final Take Home Pay	$35,250	Final Take Home Pay	$37,275
		Take home this much more......	$2,025

8. Home Base Business Tax Deductions

Want to reduce your tax burden today? Then start a home-based business for fun, profits, and hefty tax deductions. A home base business can be very beneficial in helping you share the cost of your household expenses. Tax deductions are very similar to that of a regular business however, as a home base business you are sharing the cost of running your business with your regular home expenses resulting in tax deductions. The golden rule: **all business expenses are deductible provided they are ordinary and necessary in operating your business for profit**. That's it. So, if you are the owner of an ice house, a Russian Ballerina might not pass as ordinary and necessary to operate your business but a car, computer, home office, contractors, employees, utilities, insurance, travel expenses and on and on are all deductible business expenses which are ordinary and necessary in operating your business. Get it?

Small Business Self-Employment Taxes 50% Deduction

Most people start their small business from their home with the intention of growing it to a big business one day. Microsoft was started from a home car garage. However, as your business began to earn money the business owner is faced with another reality and that is self-employment taxes. As an employee 50% of your FICA or Social Security and Medicare taxes are paid for you by your employer and sent to the IRS for you. Now that you are a sole proprietor, freelancer, or independent contractor you must pay your own taxes on your net earnings. The Self Employment tax is paid in two parts: 1). 12.4% Social Security taxes for 2016. This amount is limited to the first $118,500 of your earnings. 2). The second part is for

Medicare taxes which you will pay an additional 2.9% on all net earning without a limit like the Social Security tax. This brings your total tax due on earning to a whopping 15.3%.

To offset this tax burden the IRS has allowed you to deduct 50% of these taxes to reduce you AGI or taxable income. For example, if your self-employment taxes are $5,000, you can claim 50% or $2,500 as a tax deduction and reduce your taxable income. This deduction is allowed to you whether you itemize or take the standard deduction or not. It doesn't matter you still get the deduction and pay less taxes.

Examples of Home Based Business Tax Deductions

Home Office Deduction:

The home office deduction allows you to deduct or expense a portion of your home expenses related to operating a home-based business possibly reducing your tax burden. As an example, you can deduct from taxable income: home depreciation, home repairs, certain utilities (electric, communication, internet access etc.) and mortgage interest or a portion of your monthly rent. You can deduct a portion of your homeowners insurance and real estate taxes that are dedicated to your home office.

Example: Mr. Smith an accountant prepares taxes for his clients in his home. He has an office in his home where he only conducts his business daily. As a result, he is allowed to deduct a portion of his mortgage interest for his home office on his tax returns reducing his taxable income. He can use the simplified home office deduction or he can use the actual expense method form 8829 and calculate the deduction based on the amount of space he uses exclusively for his business. Say, Mr. Smith uses 15 % of his home for business purposes only, then he can deduct 15% of his rent payments or mortgage interest and reduce his taxable income. The result is he pays less taxes.

Note: that the IRS has created a strict definition as a filter to review your home office expenses. it's called the home office test. This test is related to the location or space in which **you _regularly and exclusively_** use to conduct business or meet clients and customers. So you must past this test to claim a legitimate home office deduction. Review the IRS Pub 587.

BUSINESS EXPENSES CAN BE CLAIMED IF YOU DON'T QUALIFY FOR A HOME OFFICE DEDUCTION

The benefit of qualifying for a home office deduction is that you can get a bigger tax deduction because you can deduct a portion of your home expenses i.e., mortgage, rents, home depreciation, utilities etc. These deductions must be ordinary, reasonable, and necessary for operating your business. These tax deductions include: office expenses, supplies, business phone lines, computers, furniture etc. As long as it is used for a portion of your business you are allowed a tax deduction expense for the portion of business use. So keep detail records of the use percentage. You are allowed to deduct as a business expense, auto mileage or auto depreciation as well. Discuss this with your tax professional to ensure that you are taking all legal tax deductions and that you are keeping good records of your transactions. Below is a sample of major expense categories deductions that are available to the home-based business owner:

Marketing and Advertising: As a business owner you can deduct advertising and marketing costs. These include business cards, brochures your letter head and all such related to the promotion of your business. You are allowed as a deduction all cost for joining professional networking organizations, car mileage or auto expense, other forms of travel to get to the shows, meeting and conventions are all deductible. You can deduct dues and fees to attend these events as well. Other deductible costs are cost related to your business website, and business communication and phone lines.

Materials and Supplies: All supplies and materials used in the production of your goods are deductible. Example: If you are a painter and sell your paintings at craft shows. You can deduct all paints, papers, brushes, and displays are all tax deductible. You can also deduct all supplies such as mailing materials, stamps, printer cartridges, pencils, paper, staplers and staples, etc. Just remember to keep detail sales receipts and records of your expenses for tax purposes.

Office Equipment: The purchase price of all equipment that you use in the operation of your business is tax deductible. This includes office furniture, computers, printers, fax machines, and phone lines etc. All tax deductible.

BUSINESS TAX DEDUCTIONS FOR YOUR CHILDREN

Employ your children, teach them lifetime skills, and get a bigger deduction from your taxable income while doing it. You must be a sole proprietor of your own business and hire your children (under the age of 18) in jobs that they can easily perform. Because your children are less than 18 years old they can be paid $6,300 which is the 2016, standard deduction and pay zero federal income taxes. This will give you the benefit of deducting the child's wages as a business expense for your business and you pay less taxes as well.

To keep this on the up and up you must keep a record or timesheet of the date, hours worked and the tasks performed. Make sure that you pay them by check and deposit the check into a bank account in the child's name or a retirement plan IRA, Roth, or a state college plan 529. These are all ideal ways to invest the children's money for their future and you get a business expense tax deduction.

Example: Tom and Sue a married couple in the 25% tax bracket is a sole proprietor in their own business. They can hire their two boys 14 and 16 years old to work in the business. They pay the two boys $6,300 each, this works out to be a tax deduction of $12,600 ($6,300 x 2), for a return of $3,150 ($12,600 x .25) in your pocket.

STRATEGY #3
REDUCE YOUR TAXES WITH THE BIG FIVE CREDITS

Tax credits are like tax deductions on steroids! While tax deductions reduce your taxable income on a percentage basis, tax credits cut your actual taxes dollar for dollar. Another way to put It, a tax deduction is worth more to you as your income grows. If your tax bracket is 10% then every dollar of deductions that you receive can cut your actual taxes by only 10 cents. While someone in the 33% tax bracket, every dollar of deduction that they receive cuts their taxes by 33 cents. So the higher your taxable income the more tax deductions are worth. Credits are different: every dollar of credits you take cuts your actual tax bill by the full dollar. Tax credits are worth more in the lower tax brackets.

Example: If you were in the 10% tax bracket, you'll need $10,000 in tax deductions to equal that $1,000 credit. On the other hand, If you were in the 33% tax bracket you will need $3,030.30 in tax deductions to get the same tax break as a $1,000 credit. Let's take a look at the five biggest tax credits that are available to you.

1. SAVERS TAX CREDIT

The Government will pay you to save for your retirement! Save money in a retirement plan and get a free tax credit from the government to help you save. The Savers Tax Credit allows you to take a credit for making contributions to an eligible IRA or other qualified retirement plans. The credit can increase from $1,000 for single filer to $2,000 for a married filing jointly filers. The eligible income ranges from a maximum of $30,750 for single filers, $46,125 for head of household filers up to $61,500 for married filing jointly filers. To qualify for the Savers Tax Credit a flier must meet certain requirements: 1) Must be at least 18-years-old. 2) Cannot be a full-time student. 3) Must not be claimed as a dependent on another taxpayer return. 4) Made contributions to a qualified retirement plan during the tax year for which the credit is claimed and, 5) Meet certain AGI income requirements.

Congress designed the credits as to allowed the taxpayer with the least amount of income to qualify for the most amount of the credits. The amount of your credit is based on a scale of 50%, 20% and 10% on the first $2,000 ($4,000 if married filing jointly) contribution to your IRA, 401k or other qualified retirement plans. The maximum credit allowed based on your income and contribution:

Contributions	Percentage	Amount to be claimed
$2,000	50%	$1,000
$2,000	20%	$400
$2,000	10%	$200

However, there are Adjusted Gross Income Phase out maximums below:

Credit allowed for your contribution	Married Filing Jointly AGI	Head of Household AGI	Single AGI
50%	$37,000 or less	$27,750 or less	$18,500 or less
20%	$37,001 - $40,000	$27,751 - $30,000	$18,501 - $20,000
10%	$40,001 - $61,500	$30,001 - $46,125	$20,001 - $30,750
0%	greater than $61,500	greater than $46,125	greater than $30,750

Example: David a married plumber will file a joint return for 2016. His income for that year was $35,000. David made a $1,100 contribution to his IRA which reduced his income and AGI to $33,900. David has met all of the IRS requirements to be eligible for this Savers Tax Credit. Based on his income and filing status, see the table above, David can take a 50% credit or $550 for his $1,100 IRA contribution. This credit reduces his taxes and puts money back into his pocket.

2. THE EARNED INCOME TAX CREDIT

The Earned Income Tax Credit (EITC) is called a refundable tax credit or what I call a negative tax credit. What this means is that if you qualify you can get money from the government when you file your taxes even if you paid zero in taxes. This credit is an attempt by the government to redistribute wealth from higher income earners to families that can use a little help. It's available to workers who earn lower levels of income or families that was employed but suffered a job lost during the tax year. The credit differs from most credits in that all credits are designed to reduce your actual tax bill dollar for dollar. For example, if you owe the IRS $500 but you are eligible to receive $1,200 worth of tax credits, the $1,200 will eliminate your $500 tax bill however, you don't get the keep the remaining $700 worth of credits. But, if you are eligible to receive this EITC you can actually owe zero in taxes and still are allowed to receive the $1,200 or more depending on your income, filing status and children from the IRS. In other words, you can actually get a refund for money that you never paid.

To qualify for the EITC you must have earned income from an employer or self-employment income. Also, if you receive unearned income from investments over $3,400 for 2016, this can disqualify you from receiving the credit. You will also be disqualified by filing married filing separately. So, check with your tax preparer for age limits and other rules for qualification for this credit. Income earners with qualifying children receives the largest amount of credits while families with no children receives the least. See the table below for maximum payouts. Notice that earners without children have a maximum credit available of $506, while the maximum credits for families with 3 or more children are as high as $6,259. The credits are designed to help working families with children, see below:

The IRS earned income limits qualifications and payments

Number of children to qualify for credit	Maximum Payment	Earned income limits for Married filing jointly	Earned income limits for Single and Head of Household
No children	$506	$20,430	$14,880
1	$3,373	$44,846	$39,296
2	$5,572	$50,198	$44,648
3 or more	$6,269	$53,505	$47,955

3. THE CHILD TAX CREDIT

Beginning in 1998, taxpayers are allowed to take this tax credit based solely on the number of eligible dependent children. This Credit was created to help pay for some of the expenses that comes with child rearing. The Child Tax Credit is one of several family friendly provisions that was added to the tax laws. To be eligible for the credit, the child must be under age 17, a U.S. citizen, and claimed as a dependent, as well as meet certain other IRS test based on current guidelines such as: the child's relationship, support, and residence. Also, you may be able to claim an Additional Child Tax Credit, only If the amount of your Child Tax Credit exceeds the amount of the income taxes that you owe.

Maximum Credit and Phase outs: According to the current IRS guidelines, the maximum credit available is $1,000 per child. The available credit is phased out for higher income taxpayers beginning when the AGI reaches $110,000 for joint filers ($55,000 for married filing separately) and $75,000 for single and Head of Household taxpayers. The credit is phased out by $50 for each $1,000 of AGI above the threshold amount. Since the maximum credit amount available to tax payers depends on the number of qualifying children, the income level at which the credit is phased out completely also depends on the number of children qualifying for the credit.

Example: Tom and Jenny is married and file a joint return claiming their two children, ages 10 and 12 as dependents. Their AGI for 2016, is $122,400. Tom and Jenny's available child tax credit for 2016, is $1,380, computed as their maximum credit of $2,000 ($2,000 x 2 children) reduced by a $620 phase out computed as their $122,400 AGI is an excess of the $110,000 threshold, the maximum credit must be reduced by $50 for every $1,000 above the threshold amount $50 x ($122,400 - $110,000/$1,000). Thus, the credit reduction equals $620 ($50 x 12.4). So Tom and Jenny's child tax credit is $1,380 for 2016.

4. The Child and Dependent Care Credit (CDCTC)

You may qualify for a maximum $3,000 credit for one child and up to $6,000 for two children or qualified dependents. This credit is allowed for taxpayers who incur employment-related expenses for the care of children, and adults that qualifies as dependents or incapacitated spouses. The credit works based on a specified percentage of expenses incurred to enable the taxpayer to work or to seek employment. Expenses on which the credit for the child and dependent care expenses are based are subject to limitations. The credit for child and dependent care expenses are allowed up to 35% of your expenses that you paid to take care of the dependent.

Example: Susan paid $6,000 in child care or dependent care expenses while she looks for full time work. She is allowed the maximum 35% of her expenses and she can receive a $2,100 credit.

Qualifications: To qualify you must file as single, head of household, married filing jointly or widower with a child as a dependent. For families with an AGI over $43,000 the credits percentage drops to 20%.

Example: Susan per the example above has $6,000 of related child or dependent care expenses. Based on the 20% credit, she can receive a credit of $1,200.

Eligibility: To be eligible for the credit an individual must maintain a household for either of the following:

- A dependent under age 13
- A depended or spouse who is physically or mentally incapacitated

5. EDUCATION CREDITS

THE AMERICAN OPPORTUNITY TAX CREDIT (AOTC)

If you are enrolled full time or half time you can qualify for as much as $2,500 as a credit to reduce your taxes. Also, the IRS will pay you and send you a check for as much as 40% of this credit up to $1,000 whether you owe taxes or not. This credit is available to offset qualified education expenses for students for the first four years of post-secondary education.

To receive the full credit your modified adjusted gross income must be $80,000 or less for single, head of household, or qualifying widow(er). $160,000 for married filing jointly. However, phase outs start at over $80,000 but less than $90,000 or over $160,000 but less than $180,000 for married filing jointly per the IRS. To qualify for the credit, you must incur school related expenses such as required fees for universities, colleges and trade school enrollment, course materials and tuition fees. Unqualified fees include: medical expenses, insurance, room and boarding, transportation etc. These expenses do not qualify for the AOTC credit.

THE LIFETIME LEARNING CREDIT (LLC)

You are allowed a credit to reduce your taxes as much as 20 percent of $10,000 for qualified school expenses or a maximum of $2,000 per year. Unlike the AOTC credit which is limited to the first four years of post-secondary education, the LLC is available for courses necessary to improve your job skills as well as undergrad, and graduate courses. Furthermore, there are no limits to the number of years that you can claim the LLC credit.

Per the IRS, to receive the full $2,000 credit your modified adjusted gross income (MAGI) which is your AGI with certain deductions added back, must be $55,000 for single, head of household, or qualifying widow(er) or $110,000 for married filing jointly. Also, just as the AOTC credit, there are certain phase out income levels for this LLC, which includes: If your MAGI is over $55,000 but less than $65,000 (over $110,000 but less than $130,000 for married filing jointly), you receive a reduced amount of the credit. If your MAGI is over $65,000 ($130,000 for joint filers), you cannot claim the credit.

PHASE 3:
INVEST IN THINGS THAT PAY YOU INCOME

RETIREMENT MONEY- INCOME FOR LIFE WITHOUT WORKING

ASK NOT *WHAT* TO INVEST IN, BUT ASK, *WHY* ARE YOU INVESTING IN THE FIRST PLACE?

I F YOU KNOW <u>why</u> you must invest, then the <u>what</u> to invest in, comes easy. As I see it, there is only one reason to invest your money, and that is to create an income for life without working. This is true financial freedom. So, the what to invest in: things that goes up in value and pay you income, comes easy. Passive income, or income that you don't have to work for is the only reason you should be investing your retirement money. Income makes you wealthy and free. You are not investing for assets, capital gains, quarterly profits, return on equity, or any of that stuff. You are going to need income for life without you having to work for it. This is true freedom. This is your ultimate goal, income for life without working.

Everybody is working for money but the problem with working for money is that when you stop working, the money stops, the savings stops, the health and life insurance stops, everything stops, and if you are not prepared you are left all alone, broke, then panic sets in. No, there is a better way to think about your financial future. *Don't be scared, be prepared!* Currently 76% of Americans are working paycheck to paycheck with no savings and our money going straight to pay taxes and to the creditors. Now how do you think we got there? Because we are programmed by the system to be consumers.

To escape this rat race, you must adhere to principals and laws just like gravity they work every time no matter who applies them. The three step guiding principles: 1) Spend less than you earn 2) Pay less taxes on what you earn 3) Invest what you earn for income. Benjamin said it best: *your money must make money, and the money that your money makes must make more money.* Keep in mind that passive income is the kind of income that you don't have to work for. It's the only income that works for you!

YOU ARE NOT GOING TO GET A PENSION FROM YOUR EMPLOYER

You are going to work for 40 to 50 years of your life, and your employer is not required to provide you a pension so you can retire. You get nothing from them, not anymore! All you get is all you have saved and invested in your 401k plan. The Employee

Retirement Income Security Act of 1974 or ERISA as it's called, is a federal law that creates basic standards for pension plans established by your employer. These plans provided you income for life after you retired from working just like social security. **However, ERISA does not require your employers to establish a pension plan for you**. Nor does it require that retirement plans provide a level of benefits. ERISA only regulates the operation of pension plans once they have been created by your employer. The Act, protects working Americans by ensuring that funds placed in retirement plans during your working years will be there when you retire.

There are two main types of plans: Defined benefit (DB) plans and defined contribution (DC) plans. DB plans are based on years of service, salary and other factors established by the employer. DC plans are based on the amount of contributions and investment performance made by the employee and employer over your years of employment.

Before ERISA, many employers DB pension plans required long years of service before employees could claim the benefits or become vested. However, most often these pre-ERISA plans would provide no benefits to employees who left their employment before a specified retirement age like 60 or 65 years old.

After 1974, employers began to shift the responsibility from themselves providing you a pension plan on to you. **This means that your employer will no longer provide you a pension and they are not required to provide you a pension by law. Ultimately you are responsible for your own pension plan. So, all you get is all you save!** If you don't learn how to save and invest your money for your retirement years, you will have nothing and will be forced to become a greeter at Walmart when you are 70 years old.

Soon after 1974, employers began to shift away from defined benefit (DB) plans where corporations used financial and actuarial models to provide you an annuity or guaranteed retirement income to a defined contribution (DC) plan. The DC makes you responsible for providing your own retirement income. These DC plans gave rise to the 401k plans that you currently have if you are lucky enough to work for a corporation that provides one. The biggest problem for you is that even though our elected officials allowed corporations to shift the responsibility from them on to you, they neglected to provide you a financial education. This is the reason that you do not have any money. It's not your fault. Our elected officials have put us into this situation. Since we were not given a financial education Wall Street spotted an opportunity and created a whole new army of financial advisors and planners that charges us more fees to manage our fee infested 401k retirement plans. So, all you get is all you save for the rest of your life. Think about that!

HOW TO CREATE YOUR OWN PENSION

A pension is no more than a steady stream of income that you cannot outlive. The idea of creating your own pension is by using these 401k, 403b, 401a, 457 or IRAs etc., retirement plans then converting this lump sum of money saved and invested over your working years into a stream of income. These 401k tax sheltered long-term saving and investment vehicles are sponsored by your employer. Companies offer these retirement plans as a way for them to attract and retain top talented people. The government puts a cap on the amount that you can invest in these plans and receive a tax deduction. The amount increases every year to reflect the rise in infla-tion. If you work for a large corporation, they will most likely add money or match a certain potion of your contribution to your account. If your employer does not offer a retirement plan, then you can invest in an IRA on your own.

Creating wealth and income from these retirement plans should be a simple straightforward strategy that is safe and let you sleep at night. The government protects these plans by creating agencies such as the Securities Investors Protection Act. Retirement plans are insured up to $500,000 per account for occurrences as brokerage insolvency, fraud and theft etc. There is no protection for market swings and losses in values of your shares. You should go to the SEC website and learn more.

There are several types of saving and investment choices in these plans. All you need is some basics of how they work and leave the rest to these plans. You don't have to be an expert to invest in a retirement plan. There are three types of mutual fund plans that are typically offered to you: 1) Cash or money markets mutual funds. Cash accounts typically do not fluctuate in value and therefore you typically should not lose any of your money or principal in these plans. They may be called a stable value dollar fund in your retirement accounts. These funds offer very little interest like a bank account but your cash is protected from market swings. A lot of savers think that if they place their money in these low interests bearing plans that there is no re-turn. Well not so fast, the truth is that if you invest $1,000, and you are in the 25% tax bracket this equates to a 25% return or $250 returned to you through tax deductions.

Along with the cash accounts just discussed, there are 2) Company stock purchasing plans, 3) Stock and, bonds mutual funds. The biggest point that I want to make is that these plans offer you easy access to several types of mutual funds. I never recommend that you invest only in single shares of stocks to include your employer stock. Why? Because, your employer can go out of business and take your money with it. Therefore, I never recommend buying a single share of stock.

Mutual funds are like any other type of business only that they specialized in buying and selling stocks in the fund. This is great because since you are not an expert you can invest in a company like a mutual fund that is in the business of making money for you. The more money they make the more you get after they take their cut. So, in this way you do not have the burden of being an expert in investing your hard earned money.

Traditional IRA contributions are tax deductible on both state and federal tax returns for the year you make the contribution, while withdrawals in retirement are taxed as ordinary income tax rates.

Roth IRAs provide no tax break for contributions, but earnings and withdrawals are generally tax-free when certain conditions are met. Such as, funds must be held for at least 5 years. If you make a withdrawal before age 59 and ½ and the withdrawal is limited to your contributions then no taxes are due. But if your withdrawals are above your contributions then taxes are due on the amount above your contributions. *However, the IRS will allow withdrawal for certain conditions such as higher education expenses, home purchases, and certain hardship situations*, Finally, if you make a withdrawal after 59 and ½ no taxes are due. These are considered retirement withdrawals.

Tax-deferred shelters: *a tax-deferred savings opportunity such as your retirement plans: IRAs, 401k, 403b etc., is one of the major ways for the average working American to reduce their taxes and create wealth at the same time with the IRS help.* You pay no taxes today when you contribute to the fund so more of your money is working for you, money making money. However, you are taxed as ordinary income when you begin to make your withdrawals in retirement. The trick is that you will most likely be in a lower tax bracket than you were when you made your contributions to the fund, thus making this a win-win for you. Below is a table of tax deferral accounts. If you are not investing in any of these types of tax deferral plans, then you are paying more in taxes than necessary. So, make sure that you or your employer are invested in one of these plans below.

2016 RETIREMENT PLANS		
Retirement plans tax reduction accounts	Plan contribution limit	Additional tax savings contributions for people age 50 and older-catchup
401(k), 403(b) and 457	$18,000	$6,000
SIMPLE IRA	$12,500	$3,000
Self employed-QRP/Keogh and SEP-IRA	20% of net self-employment income (or 25% of compensation) up to $53,000	None
Individual 401(k)	20% of net self-employment income (or 25% of compensation) plus $18,000, up to $53,000	$6,000
Traditional IRA and Roth IRA	$5,500	$1,000

Source: IRS.

Example: An Accountant earns $80,000 annually can look forward to paying nearly 50% in federal, FICA, state, and local taxes. That's nearly $40,000 in taxes. If this Accountant's investments had generated this income in a retirement plan, he would save $40,000 in taxes up front. In fact, if that extra saving of $40,000 compounding yearly for him in a retirement account that generates 8% over the next 20 years, that's an extra $2,016,734 in self-made wealth. You see understanding tax rules pays.

Look at it again, an extra 2 million dollars simply because he earned this money in a tax-sheltered retirement account that allowed his money to be sheltered from income tax and allowed him to compound his growth. You see if you have earned income from a job, you will pay approximately 50% in taxes. This will stunt your compound growth! If you invest in a retirement plan, you pay "0" in taxes until you begin making withdrawals. Now, tell me again, what should you be doing to create wealth? Correct, investing in taxed sheltered investments accounts.

THE BIG THREE THINGS THAT PAY YOU INCOME

In this section, we will narrow our focus to three asset classes that ultimately provides financial security and freedom from work. The criteria for our investment dollars are:

1. Produce income for life

2. Asset appreciation

3. Reduction in your taxes

4. Low risk of total loss of your investment

5. Use OPM or the bank's money

FIRST LET'S DEFINE YOUR RISK PERSONALITY TYPE

I believe that there are just three types of people when it comes to investing money. These three types of risk takers can form the root of our problem when it comes to investing for financial security and freedom. However, once you realize why you are investing in the first place your risk tolerance becomes less important and the financial goal that you are investing for becomes most important. Investing for financial security for your future has very little to do with taking large risk. Safety and security are the most important attributes of investing to become financially secured. For the most part these three different types of risk taker allow us to gravitate toward the investments that we feel best suits our personality type. Maybe you will see yourself progressing from one stage to the next as I did.

Savers: We all probably started as savers, this person is just not interested in taking to many chances with their money. Preservation of principal and safety is their number one concern. The best type of investing for these people is a saving account either at a bank or in their 401k retirement plans. However, they realize that they just can't create any lasting wealth as a saver because time and inflation will erode their principal and profits over time and they will always be just starting on the road to wealth and never getting there.

Speculators: So the next level that we go is the speculators. At this stage, we began to risk some money say in our 401k stock mutual fund or investing in individual stocks for a quick gain. The speculator may began trading or investing other assets for a quick gain. Say he may buy a fixer upper house then flip it for a quick profit. These people are not committed to any specific investment type they are looking to diversify and invest in a number of assets for the quick buck. On the other hand, they may diverse into different types of stocks, bonds, and commodities. These people are hoping that diversification will bail them out just in case one area does not work out. What these people want is more control over their destiny to create money they realize that they have to risk something to make something. However, they realize that they are creating money not wealth. Remember wealth is a steady stream of income for life that you don't have to work for. The speculator will have to continue trading stocks or flipping houses to create the money that they need. Finally, to create lasting wealth we move to the Specialist or the Expert.

Specialist/Expert: The specialist or the expert is very knowledgeable in one asset class i.e. real estate and this is where they invest. Why? Because, they have more knowledge about a particular asset class than anybody else does. The experts like Steve Wynn who only builds hotels and casinos, or Steve Jobs and Bill Gates in technology; they do not invest in any other area. In fact, the risk is lower because they know all of the ups and down in their specialty. The specialist is where true wealth can be created because you are able to choose the type of asset that will go up in value over time and provides a steady stream of income for life without working.

Let's turn our discussion to the three major investable asset classes.

THE THREE THINGS: MAJOR TYPES OF ASSET CLASSES THAT PAY YOU INCOME

ASSET	TYPE	Banks will loan you money (OPM)	Pay less taxes on income	Go up (appreciates) in value over time	Provide income without working	√ CHECK WHERE YOU INVEST NOW
Paper	Retirement accts, stocks, dividends, bonds, royalties from book publishing, licensing a patent, annuities, etc.	No	Yes	Yes	Yes	
Real Estate	Rentals	Yes	Yes	Yes	Yes	
Business	Distribution/ Dividends	No	Yes	Yes	Yes	

Listed above are the three major "Asset" classes that we will review in this section. Its "Type" of asset within the class breaks down each asset. Next, the assets are reviewed based on its ease of using OPM (other people's money) the banks money. Finally, we will look at whether the assets are tax favored meaning income can be used to reduce, defer or shelter certain income from taxes.

Ok let's continue. So make your selection as to where you are going to invest your money.

let's talk a little about the pros and cons of each class. For the "Paper Asset" category, we will use the retirement plans for our pros and cons review. Again, we are educating the average American and the average American has access to a retirement plan.

HOW PAPER ASSETS PAY INCOME

Portfolio Income: Portfolio income is generated basically from the sales of assets i.e stock, bonds, currencies, commodities, antiques collectibles, cars, real estate that you flip for a quick profit. In other words, income is generated when you buy at one price and sell at a higher price. You know the buy low sell high speculator personality. This income can be taxed differently depending on what went on in your investments that year. It's suited for the speculator or gamblers the day trader that buys and sells stock intra-day. You have to ask yourself did my investments generate interest income. If yes, then this income will be taxed as ordinary income and taxes can be as high as 43.4% depending upon your income. This includes a new 3.8% Medicare tax for high income earners. Another question is: did you sell all or a portion of the investment? If yes, then this is a capital gain or loss. These sales can be short term in nature meaning if held shorter than 12 months then it's taxed as ordinary income.

If held longer than one year it can be taxed as capital gain or loss based on a tax bracket as low as 0%, 15% and 20% and a 3.8% Medicare tax for high income earners. However, you do not pay social security taxes on these investments. An additional benefit of capital gains is that it can be used to offset a certain amount of capital losses on other investments. However, the biggest disadvantage that I had to deal with, was that the banks would not lend me money to speculate. So, I had to come up with my own money to buy the assets, and on top of that I had zero control over my money once I place that bet. The market either will take your money or give you money. I could not see my way to financial freedom this way.

However, others like Mr. Buffet obtain financial freedom through portfolio income. You probably have heard the stories about investor Billionaire Warren Buffett. He is claimed to pay a lower tax rate than the majority of earned income Americans because federal taxes on his investment income (portfolio) is lower than the taxes most Americans pays on earn (salary and wage) income. Since practically all of Warren Buffett income comes from his investments, he is legally able to pay a lower income tax rate on his income than his secretary. For 2015, the top tax rate on portfolio income is just 23.8% for long-term capital gains; however, it's 43.4% on income from earned income.

HOW BONDS PAY INCOME

Bonds are debt instruments or more commonly called IOU's or loans that you the lender, make to an institution: government (federal, municipal) or corporation etc. The funds are used to fund normal operations or invest in some project or other activity. They do pay regular income so that is why it's worth taking a look at them. Remember the goal, income without working. Individual bonds or bonds mutual fund can be purchased from most major brokerage firms on the web, also you can purchase bond funds through most 401k retirement plans as well.

There are several classes of bonds but for our purpose of producing a steady stream of income we will focus on what I call the 3 majors. All bonds generally operate similar but are used for different purposes. However, in this presentation we are looking at producing an income money machine an investment that pays you money safely, while you sleep. Keep in mind that the most important feature of a bond is the entity that issued it. Our first priority as an income investor is **a return _of_ our money not a return _on_ our money.** Preservation of capital is key. So keep that in mind. With that let's take a look.

Below are 3 major bonds categories that's maybe worth your consideration for income:

1. Treasury/savings bonds
Treasury bonds are issued with the highest credit rating to finance the budgets and deficits of the federal government. The interest income is taxable at the federal level and tax-free at the state and local levels.

2. Corporate bonds
An investment grade corporate bond has healthy financial statements and are rated by the major rating agencies i.e. Moody's and Standard and Poor's. Corporations issue these bonds to fund their operations. They pay a higher yield than treasury bonds however, they are taxable at the federal and local state levels.

3. Municipal bonds
Municipal bonds or "munis" are issued by states, local governments, and their agencies. They can be investment-grade or high-yielding bonds depending on the credit rating of the issuing state. The interest income is tax-free at the federal level and can be tax-free at the state level if you live in the issuing state. Below consider the tax effect of investing in muni tax-exempt bonds vs. a taxable corporate bond.

Example: Say, if you had $25,000 to invest for income and your choices were a 5%, tax-free muni or taxable 7%, corporate bond, which investment would be better for you? See below where you would be better off with the tax exempt muni vs. the taxable corporate bond even though the corporate bonds pay you more income and a higher interest rate. After the calculation, you see that the after tax yield is 5% on the muni and 4.7% on the 7% taxable bond.

Net effect of Federal Income Taxes on Tax-Exempt vs. Taxable bond yields		
	Tax-exempt 5% Bond	Taxable 7% Bond
Your Investment	$25,000	$25,000
Interest Income	$1,250	$1,750
Federal income tax rate 33%	$0	$578
Net income return	$1,250	$1,173
After taxes yield on investment	5.00%	4.70%

Note: If you are subject to the Alternative Minimum Tax (AMT), you may have to include interest income from municipal bonds in calculating your taxable income.

If you are going to invest in bonds, you want to get familiar with some of the terms associated with bonds:

Coupon: Bonds can be called an income money machine because of this coupon feature. Bond coupons can pay you income regularly and predictably without you working. You receive this interest income payment from purchasing the bond. The borrower or issuer pays you this coupon over the life of the bond. Say if you buy a 5 year $1,000 corporate bond that pays you 7% biannually then you can expect to receive $70 every 6 months for 5 years unless the bond is cancelled or called.

The Date of Issue: This is the date that the bond begins to pay you interest income (money machine).

Maturity date: This is the date that you will get your money back or the amount that you paid for the bond. Say if you bought a 5-year bond with a face value of $1,000, then on your 5th year anniversary depending on if the institution is solvent or didn't go bankrupt, you will get your $1,000 returned to you. Also you can sell your bond before its maturity date or even buy a bond before it matures, however the value that you receive or pay may differ from the face amount of the bond. This buying and selling before the bond matures can result in a capital gain or loss. So talk to your broker.

Maturity value: This is the face value or par value amount that the borrower will pay you the holder of a bond on the maturity date. Say if you bought a $1,000 face or par value bond then the maturity value that you will receive is $1,000.

Yield to Maturity: When you purchase a bond after the date of issuance the yield to maturity may be different than the coupon payments. That's because the bonds are traded on the open market like a stock and the bond price can go up or down and fluctuate with the market affecting the coupon payout income stream.

Example: You purchased a $1,000 corporate bond with a coupon of 5% and 10 years to maturity. Then, in 3 years into the bond, the company is earning more cash so the new buyers will have to pay $1,050 for the same bond. Remember as bond prices go up yields falls and as bond prices go down yields increase. Therefore, to calculate the yield that you are receiving you divide the coupon 5% or $50 by the new face value of $1,050 for a yield to maturity of 4.76% . See how the yield decrease from 5% to 4.76% as the bond price increase from $1,000 to $1,050? This is good for you in determining how the market will affect your bond and the yield that you will get which may be different from the coupon rate.

Callable Bond
A feature that certain bonds have allows the issuer of the bond or the company in the case of a corporate bond to call or cancel the bond before its maturity date. Therefore, your income stops. Say if the market interest rate has dropped since the company issued the bond, they may want to cancel that bond and reissue or refinance the debt at a lower interest rate. However, callable bonds usually pay more interest to you.

In addition, there are a few risks associated with the purchase of bonds. Below are just the major ones:

Interest rate risk: Single bonds and mutual bond funds Changes in the economy can cause interest rates to change. This is the same for stocks and bonds. It is important because bond prices move in the opposite direction of the interest rates. If the current interest rate drops then bond prices will increase and the value of your bond or fund will increase. However, as interest rate rises the value of your bond or fund bond will fall. Keep in mind that the value or price of the bonds changing only matters if bonds are sold before they mature. Since we are in a very low interest rate environment, interest rates will probably go up not down, I mean how low can they go in 2016?

Inflation risk: Since bonds payments are fixed income and things generally goes up, the fixed income may not keep pace with the rise in prices or inflation. The longer the term of the bond the greater the inflation risks.

Credit risk: The issuer of the bond may not be able to pay you timely or not at all. High yield junk bonds typically will have an above average credit risk because financially unstable companies issue them. This risk is avoided by purchasing U.S. treasury bonds or savings bonds because the U.S. has never defaulted.

INVEST IN SINGLE BONDS VS. BOND MUTUAL FUNDS

Investing in single bonds can be a time consuming task because you must do all of the research homework yourself. Also it can require a large sum of money to get started with the proper diversification across different bonds high and low risk categories discussed above. Notably high-risk bonds will pay more interest income and a higher yield, but they carry more risk of default as well. You may think of reducing the risk of a high yield corporate bond that pays 7% with purchasing low risk Treasury bonds. So you can spread the risk around sort-of speak. In addition, it can cost you upwards of more than $100,000 just to get started buying different classes of bond to achieve true diversification. Remember, if a high yield bond defaults, you can lose your entire investment. Treasury bonds have never defaulted. Keep in mind that a return <u>of</u> your money is better than a return <u>on</u> your money.

Investing in a bond mutual fund is less costly to get started and less time consuming. The funds are rated with risk ranging from high, moderate, or low. You can invest in a bond mutual fund and let the bond fund manager do all the work for you. Purchasing a bond fund is similar to purchasing a stock mutual fund. You can start with very little money and the fund pays you income monthly after operating expenses. You can even request to reinvest your income and purchase more shares in the fund. Bond funds have several categories like treasuries, investment grade corporate, high yield junk, municipals etc., so you can choose bond funds that very risky or very safe. The bond mutual funds management team is responsible for all of the research and daily monitoring of all of the bonds that make up the pool of bonds that makes up your investment. Again, you can purchase bond mutual funds through your 401k, and defer all taxes or just by calling one of the major brokerage companies over the web.

So make sure you understand the management style of the mutual fund that you invest in which is described in the fund's prospectus. Keep in mind that the ultimate purpose for investing in bonds or funds is to create income. Income without working and freedom of choice is the goal. Since we are in a low interest rate environment the value of your single bond or bond fund may go down. However, the coupon rate or the interest income that you receive will remain the same. If you plan to sell your bonds or funds while interest rates are rising then you can expect the value of your bond or fund to be lower than what you paid for it. So the question becomes, should I keep the lower paying bonds or sell them and buy the higher paying interest coupon bonds? In a bond fund, the management will make that decision for you. The longer the bonds maturity date the more likely the bonds value will change based on current interest rate changes. Short-term maturity bonds tend to be less sensitive to changes in the current interest rate environment.

TAXES ON BONDS

Bond income is taxable or tax-free at the federal and or local state level: **Treasury bonds** are taxable at the federal level and are tax-free at the local and state level. **Municipal bonds** income is tax free at the federal level and may be tax free at the state and local level depending on if you live in the state that the bond was issued. Income from **Corporate bonds** are taxed at both the federal, local and state levels. Keep in mind that bond income is considered passive in nature so you pay a lower tax on the income because you don't pay Social Security and Medicare or FICA taxes. In addition, you may be able to buy these bonds in your retirement account and defer taxes into the future until you start making withdrawals.

HOW STOCKS PAY INCOME

Dividends are how stocks pay you income. The correct mindset to have when you buy dividend-paying stocks in a company is that you must see yourself as a silent partner in the business. This mental shift will keep you from buying stock in a company and praying for an increase in the stock price or short-term capital gain. Keep in mind that 90% of people lose money in the stock market. Why, because they see themselves as a short term speculator. And, you know what happens to most speculators or gamblers, they lose their money. They buy and sell based on emotions and wrong timing. **They buy high and sell low. They repeat this cycle until they are broke and don't have any money left.** To make money investing in stock you must shift your mindset to being an active part owner of the company. Becoming a partner and an owner in a company is to take a business-like approach.

If I want to become a long-term part owner in a company, I will look to see if I can receive capital gains, dividend income, and reinvest my profits for additional gains while I remain invested for long periods. In other words, I want my money to make more money. If the business model and business environment favors the company, I am in for the long haul. To see myself as an owner before I make an investment in the company, I will look at the business cash flow and other financial statements. I want to make sure that cash is flowing into the business not out of it. If possible I'll visit a location like Walmart or McDonald to see how the business is being managed. I really get involved in the business because I am not just buying some stock here and hoping that it goes up without taking any interest in the company.

Dividend Paying ETF/Mutual Funds: If I don't have the time to get involved in the company then I'll just buy a dividend paying mutual fund or ETF and let the fund manager do all the work for me. There are ETF (Exchanged Traded Funds) and Mutual Funds that specializes in companies that have a proven track record of paying regular increasing dividends over many years. To get sufficient dividend income from purchasing shares of stock can require a large sum of money to purchase enough stock to pay enough in dividend income also, single stock pay dividends quarterly. Dividend paying mutual funds tends to pay dividends on a monthly basis. Since they invest in a large number of companies there is always a monthly payout going on. For more information, you can research these mutual fund/ETF companies online at any major brokerage company i.e. Vanguard, Fidelity, Schwab etc. The main reason I will invest in a dividend paying stock, ETF, or Mutual Fund is that I want to receive income and to be paid for the volatility or when the stock price goes down, I will still get the same dividend payment or income from being an investor.

There have been studies that discovered approximately 50% of a stock's total returns come from the company's ability to pay you dividends over a long period. The trick is to find companies that can raise dividends consistently. If a company can raise its dividend regularly and consistently this means that the company is profitable, and the stock price will go up. *This is how you create a dividend income money machine.* A corporation pays you your part of the profits as dividends from its earnings. In other words, a corporation must have profits or cash in the bank to pay dividends to its owners. The more shares you own in a corporation the more dividends that you receive when and if it's paid. Corporation pay dividends quarterly but dividend payments are quoted in annual terms. Say, if a company pays you a $4.00 dividend per share, you must divide the payment by 4 quarters. Therefore, your quarterly dividend distribution would be $1.00 per share per quarter. A corporation can increase, decrease, or cancel its dividend payments if necessary to keep the company afloat.

Example: Dividends can be paid on a per share basis, this means that if a corporation pays an annual $3.00 per share dividend and you own 1,000 shares of the stock then you get 1,000 x $3 = $3,000 in annual dividend payments. In addition, dividends can be paid based on the percentage of the current share price. Say a 5% dividend means that if each share is worth $20.00 you get $1 per share 5% x $20.00 = $1.00 per share. In this case, your 1,000 shares would net you a dividend income payout of $1,000.

However, not all companies pay dividends. If a company is in its infancy or growth phase, it may not want to pay its cash to you as dividends. Many tech companies do not pay dividends. Facebook and Google two of the largest companies per capital to date do not pay dividends. Instead, they use their cash to reinvest in their company's research and development for new products or they may use their cash to buy other companies as opposed to paying it out to investors. So if dividend income is what you want make sure that the companies you invest in actually have a long history of paying increasing dividends. Most companies will pay you a dividend so you can share in the profits to keep you invested in the stock. Many big matured companies will pay you a dividend to compensate you for the share price remaining flat over long periods. The shares are not producing any capital gains so they pay you a dividend to keep you invested.

TAXES ARE REDUCED ON DIVIDEND INCOME

Taxes are deferred on dividend income in a retirement account. However, taxes are paid on dividends that are in a taxable brokerage account. For tax purposes, dividends can be "qualified or unqualified". Qualified dividend can be tax free if your income falls between the 10% and 15% tax brackets up to maximum of 20% for income in the 39.6% tax brackets based on IRS requirements. However, nonqualified dividends are taxed the same rate as ordinary income currently at 39.6%. There is an additional 3.8% tax for high-income earners so check with your tax professional for the latest updates.

THE STOCK MARKET IS A WEALTH PRODUCING VEHICLE

To begin we must start with a basic premise, and that is that the stock market is a wealth producing vehicle. Once we can accept this premise we can relax and learn how to take advantage of the opportunities that the market presents to us to create wealth and financial security. There are trillions of dollars going into the stock market daily. Money is created out of thin air. There is buying and selling going on 24/7. Let me explain. If you buy a stock at $10 and it goes to $12, where did this extra money come from, did anybody lose money? No. Another person buys this stock and it goes to $14. Again, where did this extra money come from, did anybody lose money? No. Another person buy at $14 and it goes to $16. It will continue this wealth production until there is nobody else who wants to buy the stock at $16. This person cannot find anybody who want to buy at $18 and he is stuck holding it. Then people began to sell the stock and it goes to $14 and this person suffers a lost if he sells at $14. As long as he holds the stock he has an unrealized loss. Then it will fall in price until buying starts again and this wealth production process start all over again.

This buying and hoping that somebody else will buy it from you at a higher price is called the greater fool theory. It says that a price can be justified by a rational buyer under the belief that another party is willing to pay an even higher price. And no stock goes up forever. Some companies may go out of business and take your money with it. So, in this section we will only be referring to investing for the long term using S&P 500 index mutual funds not individual stocks. The S&P 500 index is a basket of the best 500 companies in America. Over the long term this market goes up. Period. In fact, as I write this, the stock market is approaching an all-time high of 20,000. The market has never created this much wealth for people that knows how to take advantage of the opportunities that it represents before. Need proof? Look at the S&P 500 stock chart below.

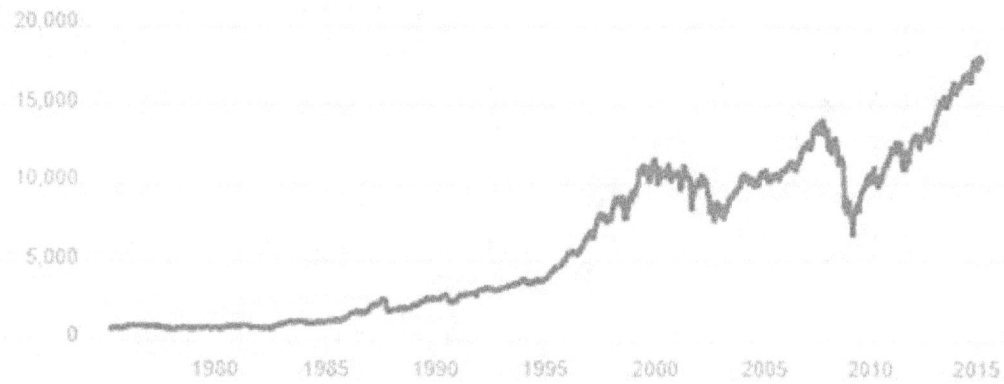

It's been said that most people miss the up swings or wealth production of the market because they fear the down swings. In other words, they are trying to time the market and second guess the market. We want to get into the market at the perfect time on the upswing and avoid the downs swings. But the market is made up of up and down swings. In fact, it is the down swings that create the value or opportunity for the up swings. The greatest wealth creation comes from being invested in the down swings.

WHEN IS THE RIGHT TIME TO INVEST IN THE STOCK MARKET?

The question that I get a lot: *"is now a good time to get into the stock market?"* Which really is a two-part question. 1) The first part of the question can be answered by "yes or no". It depends on when you need the money. If you need it in the short term say for 2 to 5 years, then no, this is not a good time for you to get into the stock market. 2) On the other hand, if you don't need the money until later in life, then "yes" now is a good time to get into stocks. Since the overall stock market makes money over a long period of time say 5 to 10 years. To prepare yourself to get ready to invest is to determine your short-term needs. The best way to handle this is to save money that you need to meet your short-term expenses in an interest-bearing account. Like a bank account or money market fund. But the rest of your investments should be going into a long-term low fee stock index fund. Any online brokerage house like Schwab, Vanguard, or Fidelity etc., can assist you with low fees index funds. To answer question #2) *Can you stick to a long-term strategy?* If you cannot stick to a long-term investing strategy, then now is not a good time to get into the market. Let this be a simple guide for you: *Never invest short term money in long term investments or the results can be ruins because you may have to pull the money out right before the market can do its part in returning you a profit over the long term. This is what I call the magic of the markets.*

YOUR FIRST INVESTMENT- *PASSIVE INDEX*

"Set it and forget it" This strategy is powerful and simple: you are always in the market invested in the long-term trend which is up.

You first investment or your bread and butter investments should be investing for your long term financial security, called passive index investing. Passive investing is simply investing long-term money into a stock index mutual fund. The fund selects the stocks for you to invest in. So, you don't have to worry about researching companies to invest in or making stock selections. Let the funds do all the work. You just set it and forget it. You should have a long-term strategy and that is to stay invested in a low cost, passive stock index mutual fund. Why? Because over the long-term passive investing will make money for you. Jumping in and out of stocks is called a trade for the short term and studies show that 95% of these people lose money trading stocks. To avoid this inevitable lost you should invest early and often and let the magic of the market make you wealthy. The biggest secret to the stock market wealth creation is time. The average American cannot make the market move and give you profits. So, we must learn to **follow the money** go with the long-term flow of the market, and that is up. We do not create the profits all we can do is to remember this formula to making money in the stock market and that is: *Buy now, then let time make you money, then sell.* This is your new mantra: Buy---time---sell.

Wealth building with these passive investment retirement plans should be simple with a straightforward strategy that allows you to sleep at night no matter what the stock market is doing. Bull or bear markets, up or down who cares. With this simple automated strategy, you will be able to increase your wealth over the long term no matter what's happening in the markets today. The best part is that you don't have to become an investment expert to create wealth using this strategy. Let the market create wealth for you. *If you stick to a simple "set it and forget it" or commonly called buy and hold **passive strategy** using low cost fees S&P 500 index stock and money market* *funds with a long term horizon, you should be just fine.* I do not recommend an **active strategy** which tries to pick the next hot stock and timing the market by buying and selling stocks to make a short term profit for the average investor. If you have a long time horizon before you retire, then your long-term passive investment strategy should be to "Buy it and hold it". For the average working American their just is no other way. This strategy works in your favor by using low fee index mutual funds.

Most of us are not skilled in trading and timing the market, so you should stick to a buy and hold investing strategy. If short term trading and market timing was so easy, then why do Wall Street hedge funds and investment brokerage firms invest billions of dollars in computer software and servers that can hack into the Wall Street stock data base real time. They can see the trade before it happens or front running it's called, and literally steal a portion of your money. They employ quant strategies, scientific algorithms, and computerized (HFT) High frequency trading systems, just to make money. Gone are the days of the stock market fundamental or technical analyst, these Wall Street crooks just hack into the New York Stock Exchange data base system and steal money and it's all legal. A long-term buy and hold strategy can protect you against these crooks because they are trading for the short term. And, in the long term that market as a whole always goes up. **This is your edge and this is how you win!**

CONTRIBUTE EARLY AND OFTEN TO A RETIREMENT PLAN

I am often asked about the maximum contribution to a 401k employer sponsored retirement plan, and is it a good investment for their money. The answer is, yes you better believe it is. The Bureau of Labor Statistics survey shows that out of the 61% of employers that offer a 401k plan half of them offers zero matching. Nothing! For those that do offer matching, the average match is a pathetic 3%. So, this is the strongest case to be made for considering Social Security as a vital part of your retirement plan. Because for the average American, it is. **Keep in mind that you are not going to get a steady stream of income or a pension from your employer to live on in retirement**. If you don't believe me then go to Walmart and see who greets you at the door. That's right, retirees. Of the few people that manage to declare retirement, most of them are not financially secured and they run out of money and can't stay retired. What a shame. Again, you are not going to get a company pension so it's all on you. The reality is all you will get is all you save.

Remember that the Retirement Plan table discussed earlier showed that the **employee maximum deductible contribution** amount is $18,000 for a person that is less than 50 years old to a 401k plan. I know most people cannot afford to invest this amount mainly because of their bulging debt loads and other expenses. Their debt load and expenses are preventing them from contributing the full $18,000 plus and additional $6,000 if you are 50 years are older for a maximum employee contribution of $24,000. But do you know that these amounts are just the employee contribution? When combined the total employee and employer contribution to your 401k can max out at $53,000 for 2016. In other words, your employer can contribute another $35,000 to your 401k If they wanted to. But they don't, they only contribute on average 3%. This leads to financial insecurity.

Example: If a plan offers an employer 50% match on 6 percent of wages that the employee contributes, then the total potential match is 3 percent. While 3% may not be too bad if you are earning a million dollars annually, but for you, according to survey, the median household income in the United States was $54,462 for 2015. This means that all you get on average is $1,643. That's it! Keep in mind that your employer can contribute up to $35,000 for you. And you need to kiss your lucky rabbit foot that you were one of the few workers that are offered a 401k plan. However, there is no law that says that your employer must contribute to your retirement plan. Your employer don't have to give you a damn thing! And looking at this 3% matching they really are not because you still must pay fees out of this. This means that Social Security will be a reality for you. We will discuss Social Security in the following chapters.

TO MAKE MONEY INVESTING YOU MUST "BUY LOW-SELL HIGH"

Now we all know how to get rich in the stock market right? Buy low and sell high. Well if this is so easy why can't anybody do it? Why is it so difficult? Because buy low sell high is against our human nature, It's counterintuitive, it's goes right against our human basic psychology of fear and greed. **To make money short term we need to buy when everybody is selling and sell when everybody else is buying**. Buy low sell high! The problem with buy low sell high is that no one wants to buy something when prices are falling (buy low) and no one wants to sell something that's going straight up in value (sell high). Instead, we do the opposite. We buy (high) when we should be selling and sell (low) when we should be buying. We repeat this cycle of "buy high – sell low" until we are broke. There must be a better way!

What prevent us from making money in the stock market over the short term is: fear and greed. When do you buy (greed) and when do you sell (fear)? No one knows. If they did, they certainly would not tell you. They would be living on their yacht in the blue waters of the Caribbean, sipping champagne and making money trading stocks. Making money short term-trading is all about our human emotions and market timing. Humans can't time the market to know exactly when to make money trading or investing. To me the emotions of greed and fear are the biggest problems that I had when I was trying to time the markets. My emotions was involved and if you ask people what is the dominate emotion that they feel in the markets it will be fear. Your fear and greed rules the markets. And, you know what acting on these emotions of fear and greed leads to in the market right? Losses! The person that learns to transcend these two emotions of fear and greed can be successful in their investing. And having a long term strategy give you this power to transcend fear and greed. To me, money is emotional, it's the most emotional thing next to love. Money is just not money, it's not just pieces of paper and coins that we give value too. Money is survival itself. Live or die.

So what's behind these emotions? Well Abraham Maslow in his hierarchy of needs described it best. That unless we take care of our basic needs of survival and safety first, they will just keep messing up our long term investing program. That's because we are scared of losing money, scared of losing our survival and safety. Remember how you felt when you lost your job unexpectedly and you needed that paycheck. You were afraid that your basic needs of survival and safety was not going to be met. Let a person lose their job which provides for their basic needs and they will start to think like an animal. So the best way to solve these needs are to take care of them first. And we have, it's called an emergency fund. This fund we discussed in the prior section is your security blanket. Therefore, when you are investing for the long-term, stay focused because you have the short-term needs covered by your emergency fund.

FOLLOW THE MONEY AND YOU'LL GET SOME

Below is a chart of a stock index fund. It represents the largest best run companies in America. So, what do we see? ***It's going up over the long term***. So, what should you be doing? Yes, following the money! Don't question it or analyze it because you cannot make sense out of it. But you do see that over the long term it goes up. Folks don't miss this. Stop listening to CNBC, Wall Street Journal or any of the money, political news channels, and magazines that you tune in to. If you listen to these folks you will lose all your money, because these so called Financial Analyst and Advisors don't know where the stock market is going. If they did they wouldn't be telling you. They would be investing and trading stocks making all the money and living on their yachts in the Cayman Islands. Why would they tell you and give you some money? They would not.

Remember this when it comes to investing your money: No one knows what you think they do! What you personally observe matters most. Look at the chart below, it's going up over the long term, period. You see it and you observed it. This is what is meant by personal observation. Your job is not to fight it, reason, analyze it or question it. Your job is to follow it. Just follow the money and you'll get some. In fact, the stock market is the highest it has ever been in history. **People do not lose money because the stock market is not making profits for them. People lose money because they pull their money out the market during the dips or corrections. In other words, they sell when they should be buying and they buy when they should be selling.** Why, because we get afraid that we are going to lose all of our money that we worked so hard for all of these years. A stock index fund should be the workhorse for your money and form the basis of your allocated portfolio.

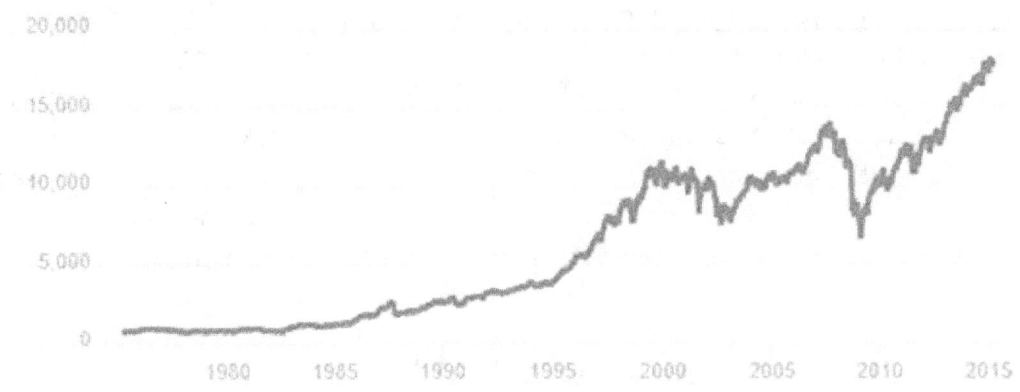

Google Finance - Yahoo Finance - MSN Money

Further, you must reinvest, diversify, automate, use dollar cost averaging, re-balancing, and let the market and time do the work for you. Set it and forget it.

Remember the market will dip or correct (go down) in the short run but over a long enough period of time, it always goes up, look at the long-term stock chart again. What do you see and personally observe? Yes, it goes up over the long term all by itself.

Below is just a very small sample of index funds with the low expense ratios or annual cost that are available to you today. These funds you can easily invest in with your employer 401k or your personal IRA. These funds created this upward climbing chart above. The stock market is a wealth producing vehicle. Just follow the money and you'll get some.

S&P 500: Invests in the 500 largest U.S. companies		
Name	Ticker	% Expense Ratio
Schwab® S&P 500 Index	SWPPX	0.09
USAA S&P 500 Index Member	USSPX	0.25
Vanguard 500 Index Inv	VFINX	0.17
Vantagepoint 500 Stock Index I	VPFIX	0.4

Reinvestment: This is basic, fundamental, and the fastest method to creating wealth. Remember money makes money and that money makes more money. To profit from a reinvestment strategy you must not spend or receive your profits in cash. Instead, you must use your profits and reinvest them to make additional purchases of shares of stocks. Make your profits make you even more money. Reinvesting the capital gains and dividends that you receive from investing in stocks funds, and interest from cash or bonds funds allows you to make more money from your money.

Tax free compounding is the most silent perpetual wealth building strategy ever created. This is tax free earnings on top of tax free earnings. What is commonly called reinvestments. What this means that if your tax-free or tax-deferred investments gains an average of 10%, then the principal you invested received 10% and the 10% interest gets 10% and so it goes forever. Money makes money and the money that money makes, makes more money and that money makes more money and on and on...True legacy wealth. It's like an ATM machine, once you get the money machine started, it can make you wealthy all by itself. If you are in the 28% tax bracket guess what? Ever buck you get to keep is just like getting a 28% return on your money! Now try getting that at your local bank. Compounding in a tax free or deferred environment makes you wealthy. The rich know this and now so do you.

Diversification: To remove our human fearful nature from our investing we must learn to diversify. This means not to risk everything on one single stock or your company's stock. However, if you choose to invest in an S&P 500 index mutual fund, your money would be spread out or diversified over 500 different companies. So diversification is taken care of for you.

Automate your contributions: This is the easy part because as you participate in a 401k or other pension plans the companies that you work for will at your request have a certain amount of money taken out of your paycheck and deposited (contributed) into the fund of your choice inside of your 401k, all taken care of for you. So all you do is sit back and create wealth over time until you are ready to take the money out.

Dollar Cost Averaging: Is a process where you select a certain amount of money that you want to automatically invest per pay period. In other words, the dollar amount that you decide to invest will stay the same and will purchase a certain amount of mutual fund or stock shares depending on the share price.

Example: Say you are investing $100 monthly and the stock or index fund price is $10 a share. The first month you will purchase $100/$10 = 10 shares. Say the next month the stock or index price rise to $20. Then your $100/$20 = 5 shares. So you see the same $100 will buy less shares when the market is going up. Say the next month the stock or index falls to $5 a share. Then your $100/$5 = 20 shares. So this month when the market is declining you are buying more shares while everybody else is panicking, selling and running for the hills.

The wealth creation comes in next month when the market goes back up and the shares that you bought at $5, now they are worth $20. This means that you have just created $15.00 of wealth per share that you own out of thin air.

Rebalancing your distributions: This is a buy low sell high long term strategy. It's a process that you use to maintain the correct portion or allocation amount of stocks, bonds, and cash that you feel comfortable with. Say if you had your money split, 40% cash and 60% stock and your total fund goes up in value to 80% stock and 20% cash you would have to rebalance your portfolio back to your desired 40% cash and 60% stock. So, you would sell some of the appreciated stock and place it into your cash fund or bond fund. You see the stock index fund is the workhorse of your investments, it creates all the profits however, the cash fund is just a holding fund. So as the stock fund goes up at rebalancing time you will sell some of the stock fund and put it into your cash fund or bond fund. So you sell the stocks when it is high and buy bonds that is low. Buy high sell low.

Example A Rebalancing Strategy: Is to *keep your age in cash and the rest in a stock index mutual fund.* There are many strategies this is just one that I used. The basis of this strategy is that stock and bonds move opposite each other. If one goes down the other goes up. Your cash fund or stable dollar does not fluctuate with the rest of the market. So cash is a good place to park your money if you don't like to see your money fluctuate up and down. **Using the age method**, say if you are 40 years old and have $10,000 invested in a 401k. You may keep 40% in cash or bonds. So, $4,000 would be in cash or bonds and 60% or $6,000 to be in a low fee stock index fund.

At year-end suppose I check my account and saw that my stock fund did very well and my total balance is now $20,000. However, I see that 90% is in stock and only 10% is in cash or bonds now. So I would sell some of my stock fund to get the percentages back to a 40/60 cash to stock split. So $20,000 x 60% = $12,000. So you rebalance by putting only $12,000 in your stock fund and $8,000 or 40%, your age (40 y/o) in your cash fund. Now you are back into alignment of your desired 40% (your age) cash and 60% stock. You can rebalance quarterly or yearly which ever works for you. So try to follow my example here and do some practice. Remember, to keep it simple here, you want to be in the stock market for the long term (your edge) this is how you make money, no need to jump in and out.

ADVANTAGES AND DISADVANTAGES TO RETIREMENT PLANS

Retirement plans are for long term saving and investing. Most large companies offer these plans as a benefit to retain employees and contribute to your retirement through matching. The IRS also contributes by making your contributions tax deductible. And time creates the increase. These plans are very easy to get into but they all have pros and cons. If your company does not offer a retirement plan, you can always open up an IRA on line at any time or just consult your bank.

The Advantages of Retirement plans

Ease of entry: In most cases, you are eligible after a certain grace period of working at the company. So inquire as to what that grace period might be. Also you may be automatically enrolled into some type of Target Date Fund. This is an automatic investment plan where the assets invested are a mixture of stocks, bonds and allocated based on a multiple of your retirement age. You can elect either not to participate or redirect your money into the particular investments that you want.

Payroll deductions: Your employer at your request will have your money taken out of your check through payroll deduction and automatically invested into the investments funds that you selected. In addition, the investment funds that you select will provide you a quarterly report on your investments performance.

Double-Deduction: Taxes will completely stop or drastically reduce your ability to become wealthy if you don't take control. However, to help you overcome this problem Congress created a double-deduction tax deferred retirement plan for you called a 401k. ***Simply stated, you are not taxed on the money that you contribute into your plan and you are not taxed on the money that your money makes or gains until you make withdrawals*. This double tax-free compounding will make you wealthy.** Benjamin Franklin said it best: ***Your money makes money. And the money that your money makes, makes more money.*** Here he was talking about compound interest. However, ***if you couple compound interest with a double-deduction tax deferral and you got yourself a real landslide in to wealthy!*** You are taxed when you make withdrawals from your retirement account. Keep in mind that the money that your money makes is all profits not your principal. So this extra profits actually pays your taxes not your principal. However, you will probably be in a lower tax bracket than you are now. But, don't worry about taxes here, you will always have to pay some type of tax. That's just the way the system operates. Right now, let's build wealth and let the government help you. The maximum employee contribution in 2015 is $24,000, $18,000 plus $6,000 if you are 50 and older. That means that you can reduce your taxable income up to $24,000 for a bigger refund.

	Before	After
Saving/Refund		
Your salary	$80,000	$80,000
Your 401k/403b contributions	$0	$24.000
Taxable Income	$80,000	$56,000
Tax bracket	25%	15%
Taxes you owe	$20,000	$8,400
Saving:		$11,600

What a deal you get to invest $24,000 and the government reduces your tax bracket and your taxable income plus give you as a savings of $11,600. Do not pass this up folks!

High contribution limits: As of 2015, 401(k) employees can contribute and receive a tax deduction on up to $18,000 annually. If you are 50 or older, you can invest another $6,000 for a total of $24,000.

COMPANY MATCHING FUNDS ARE A 100% RETURN ON YOUR MONEY INVESTED, FREE MONEY!

Matching: Most large employers provide matching money to you. This is their way of contributing to your retirement plan. The match may be 6% of your salary or whatever. Your employer is giving you free money for your retirement, take it!

Your Contribution	$24,000
Company Match ($80,000 x 6%)	$4,800
Total contribution to your plan	$28,800

Loans: These plans allow you to borrow up to a certain amount currently up to 50% or your balance or $50,000. Since it's a loan you have to make payment arrangements to pay it back into your fund and pay interest to yourself. However, if you leave your job you have a grace period to pay it back before you are penalized with extra taxes.

WORKSHEET

Things to remember   **Actions To-Do**   **Dates**

Safety: If the company goes completely out of business your funds are safe. That's because they are held in a Trust Fund that is separate from the company. So when you leave you can take your funds with you.

Social security benefits: When you reach retirement age and start to make withdrawals from your 401k you will not be penalized by the social security system. In other words, your 401k distribution will not reduce your social security payments.

THE DISADVANTAGES OF RETIREMENT PLANS INCLUDE:

Retirement plans are not without their own flaws. Here are a few to keep in mind.

Waiting periods: There can be a waiting period before you are eligible to participate in a 401k plan often it could be 6 months or more depending on your employer so check with your Benefits Counselor.

High Fees: This is where the wall-street crooks steal most of your money. There has been a lot of debate in congress concerning the full disclosure of all of the fees that we pay. Well I have not seen any meaningful changes so let the buyer beware. To keep what you earn you will have to reduce your fees this is being fees efficient. The funds may post a 8% return but after all the fees and taxes you may only get 3%. So don't be fooled. The average American is losing 1% or more of their retirement fund every year to fees.

Example: Say you have $100,000 invested in your retirement plan, the crooks are stealing at a minimum $1,000 a year from your fund. Put it another way, if you have saved $100,000 with an average 4% return over your 20 years working life and you are paying 1% in fees annually your balance would be just $180,000.

Example: If you placed your savings into a simple low fee S&P 500 Index mutual fund you can drop your fees to a quarter of a percentage. It will look like this, the same $100,000 with an average 4% return and a .25% fee structure you would have a balance of $210,000 or $30,000 more just by reducing your fees. These high fee funds are actively managed funds. Meaning that you have a bunch of managers operating the fund and they want to be paid. A passive fund has the lowest fee structure because there are no managers operating the day-to-day buying and selling of stocks in these funds. To keep what you earn, you will have to consider reducing the fees that you pay.

401k income is taxable when you make withdrawals: As soon as you begin making withdrawals from your plan, you are taxed as ordinary income. That's because your taxes was deferred until withdrawal. Early withdrawals before you reach age 59 ½ are penalized an additional 10%. So beware.

You must begin withdrawals at age 70 1/2: You are required to begin withdrawing from your plan at age 70 ½. If you are employed at age 70 ½ these withdrawals can force you into a higher tax bracket.

401(K) Hardship Withdrawals

If you have an unexpected hardship that you just can't handle financially, the IRS has developed rules for such a withdrawal from your 401k. If you take a hardship withdrawal before the age of 59 1/2, you will be subject to income tax plus a 10% early withdrawal penalty. However, there is a limited set of hardship circumstances for which you can escape the 10% penalty. So make sure you discuss this with your employer because you may not be able to contribute anything to the 401(k) for months after the withdrawal or in some cases, you may not be eligible for company matching funds. The IRS defines a hardship: unreimbursed major medical expenses, a purchase of your principal residence, payments to college tuition and expenses, payments for your rent or mortgage, funeral expenses, and unreimbursed costs to repair damage to your principal home caused by a fire or other disaster.

HOW TO TURN YOUR LUMP SUM SAVINGS INTO AN INCOME STREAM

Here you will learn how to design your very own personal plan for freedom. You can turn your lifetime savings from your retirement plans into a lifetime pension plan that provides an endless stream of income. You can design your freedom as simple or a robust as you need. ***It works like this: the less money that you need to meet your lifestyle expenses, the lower the lump sum of money that you need to save to produce the income that you need. Once you know this amount you can call it your freedom number.*** First, to get started we will need a good idea of the major expenses that you want to cover for you to become financially free. Then you can choose the items that you consider are necessary expenses to be covered forever. This is the amount of cash that your assets must be generating for you to become financially free and don't have to work anymore. So the more you can look at these expenses and reduce them the sooner you will be free to do whatever you want. This is how you *"use your money to make you free"* Once I performed this exercise and finally got my finances down to a reasonable amount, I was able to become financially free much sooner. **Ok let's get started, use your Cash flow statement that you created at "Appendix A".**

Since you have completed your Monthly Living Expense Statement, you will have to select the items that you determine to be your *major expenses to be included in your financial freedom number.* These are called your *"PROJECTED EXPENSES."* Subtract them from your total expenses and this will be the financial freedom number that you will work with throughout this book. You can always change it but we need a starting point.

Example: Say your total *"**Living Expenses Monthly**"* number is $2,300, but $800 of this is your mortgage. Well you may not have a mortgage or childcare when you plan to retire or become free, so $2,300 – 800 = $1,500 monthly is the projected expenses or freedom number. This means that you must generate $1,500 a month or multiply by 12 months equal $18,000 annually. Once you perform this analysis, becoming free is much simpler because you have a specific amount that you are working with. When I performed this exercise on my finances, I would look at my total salary and then I realized that I did not need that much because I was only living on half of that. So, that half became my freedom number. Go on take a look at your total salary and compare it to what you get to live on. I hope that you are not spending all of it, if you are we really need to talk. Again, you can change it later once you get the hang of this process. Now let's talk about my favorite subject the magic of numbers. The Multiple of 25 and the Rate of 4%.

THE MULTIPLY BY 25 AND WITHDRAWAL RATE OF 4%

There is another route to freedom that you will hear in the financial community and that I have used with success so it's worth examining here. These numbers answer the question as to how much would you need to be retired or to be considered wealthy and financially free. There are two numbers one is called the *"**multiply by 25 rule**"* and the *"**safe withdrawal rate of 4%**"*. These numbers were published by a California Financial Planner named, William Bengen (1994). *The context is one* *of annual withdrawals from a retirement portfolio containing a mix of stocks and bonds. The 4% refers to the portion of the portfolio withdrawn during the first year; it is assumed that the portion withdrawn in subsequent years will increase with the consumer price index (CPI) to keep pace with the cost of living". The rule was later further popularized by the Trinity study (1998), based on the same data and similar analysis."*

Basically, the multiply by 25 rule tells you how much money to accumulate so your accumulated savings equal 25 times your annual expenses at retirement. These numbers do not include any taxes that you must pay on your accumulated savings because taxes will be different for most of us. We will discuss taxes later.

Say you figure that your projected expenses at retirement/financial freedom is $15,000 annually. Next you multiply x 25 = $375,000. So, $375,000 is your freedom number. You must accumulate this balance in your investment portfolio or your pension plans.

You try it: Projected expenses_____ x 25 = _____
This is your freedom number.

DETERMINE THE INCOME PROVIDED BY YOUR FREEDOM NUMBER

Per William Benger, Financial Planner, the 4% safe withdrawal rate assumes that your investments with a blend of 60% large cap stocks and 40% intermediate term bonds will return approximately 4% annually adjusted for inflation over each 30-year time frames. Keep in mind that the stock market generally returns between 8 and 12% annually. I have been using 4% in my portfolio since this is widely accepted in the financial planning community. It's a good idea to go over these numbers with your financial advisor to be comfortable. This number is flexible say if you feel your annual investments will yield 10% then you may want to withdraw 5% instead of 4%. On the other hand, you figure that your portfolio will only yield 5% so maybe that year you withdraw 3%. There are no fixed rules these are just numbers that sort of give you a starting point. This is up to you and your financial professional.

Ok let's run through an example. Say your freedom number is $300,000. The 4% will tell you how much income to withdraw yearly so $300,000/4% = $7,500 annually. You can change the 4% withdrawal rate up or down depending on how your investments performs annually. But for now we are using 4%. Next we must consider inflation. It's running around 2% currently so your amount of income to withdraw plus inflation is $7,500 x 1.02 = $7,650. You can get the inflation number from the Federal Reserve website. This is just one method of calculating retirement income. I am pretty sure that there are a lot more ways to create retirement income. **Ok it's your turn:**

Start with your freedom number above:
Freedom number_____ divide by 4% equal annual income of_____.
Now adjust your annual income_____ for inflation equal x 1.02 =_____.

The Disadvantages Of The 4% Withdrawal Rule:

Taxes: Federal and state local taxes are consuming a larger part of retiree's incomes. However, the rule here does not take taxes into consideration. I suggest that you meet with your tax professional in your state so you can understand how much you will need to set aside for taxes on your fixed income.

We are living longer: The rule is based on a 30-year retirement life. However, studies show that we are living longer. Thus, running out of money must be a consideration for us.

Interest rates: Since the 4% withdrawal rate is based on a 60% stock and 40% bond allocation, it's noteworthy to remember that the rule was developed more than 20 years ago, when interest rates were much higher. Currently rates are at its lowest and this will have a negative effect on the interest rate that your bonds will produce. So, your withdrawal rate may have to be adjusted downward.

Asset allocation: The rule is based on a 60% stock allocation. However, if the stock market crash right before you plan to retire you may have to withdraw less money to meet your living expenses during the down or correcting markets.

So, with these obvious flaws, the 4% withdrawal strategy should be considered as an estimate. No rule is 100% without flaws, but this rule is a very good guide for you to use as a part of your retirement strategy. Generally social security will be there as a constant and steady stream of income for us.

That's it! We will run more numbers on the next page, but you have all you really need above.

So determine your freedom number. Use the above formula until you get the hang of it this is just rule of thumb. Your true numbers will be a little different based on the actual rate of return you are getting on your savings. Keep in mind that the stock market generally returns between 6, 8 and 12% annually over the long term. So use this rule of thumb as the number you need to be financially free. Notice I did not include any social security or any other pensions or cash flows from other sources. Nor did I include the rate of interest or gains that you are getting on your other types of savings.

Obviously the higher interest rate that you get on your saving or gains will allow you to reach your number sooner. However, for simplicity sake let's leave them out. So the math will work out better for you if you include other income payments to you. For example after reducing your unnecessary expenses, your number is $15,000 to meet your yearly expenses. You simply multiply the $15,000 by 25 = $375,000, this is your new freedom number. Again this number does not include any other income source just your accumulated savings. This is the amount that you have to accumulate to be free or retire.

If you were receiving other payments i.e. company pension, Social Security or rental income then maybe your numbers looked like this: $15,000 needed for your yearly expenses subtracted from the $10,000 that you receive from other sources such as: Social Security, rental income, or passive income sources equal $5,000. Therefore, to calculate your new freedom number amount to save should look like this; Expenses $5,000 X 25 = $125,000.

So, $125,000 not $375,000, becomes your new freedom number that you need to accumulate to be free or retire. See this number is better than the $375,000 needed once you include all other income payments coming in to you forever. So go ahead and play around with these numbers. Remember they are just rules of thumb. This mean you have to monitor your expenses to ensure you do not void the numbers. I use a spending plan to stay within my numbers. Again, you have to know what freedom means to you. For me it's having the time and money to do what I want to do.

This planning rule of 25 gave me a target to hit. That was exciting because I am goal oriented and this number was achievable. Trust me once you know your number it makes going to work putting up with other people crap a lot easier for you because now you have your "WHY". And if the number was too big I just look at my expenses and reduce them even more. Maybe that vacation twice a year is not necessary so take the expense out and reduce your projected balance number that you have to accumulate. You have to know what freedom means to you.

HOW TO "*TURBO-CHARGE*" YOUR SAVINGS AND ACHIEVE FINANCIAL FREEDOM IN HALF THE TIME!

Turbo-charge your savings by increasing your savings rate is just a method that I used to save the maximum amount of my income to reach my freedom goals *faster*. This will cut years off your time to achieve financial freedom. The more you save the sooner you will hit your freedom target. This section will guide you on what to do now at your age and retirement/financial freedom target date. This is the simple part it's just math. Since you now understand the rule of 25 and the 4% withdrawal rate as discussed in the previous section. Now you can make more assumptions with these numbers. Financial independence is all about you maximizing your current income and minimizing your projected expenses. The trick is to increase you rate of saving (turbo-charge) and reduce your life style expenses so you can become financially free even sooner. I actually developed my numbers so that I could be financially free in ten years. The discipline part is that I know that I had to increase my saving rate and reduce my expenses. Yes, this was tough for me, but I did it. I learned a very valuable lesson that 75% of the crap that I was buying I did not even need. It was just stuff, that I thought I needed to make me look cool. So I eliminated a lot of my expenses and took the same money and begin to pour into my pension plan. I maxed out my 401k and with the company matching and tax breaks that I received helped me along to reach my number sooner.

WORKSHEET

Things to remember	Actions To-Do	Dates

My percentage of saving or saving rate was 35% of my income or $25,000 yearly. My target date was 10 years. So the more you can save the quicker you can become financially free. If you were to save 50% or 70% of your earning you can reduce the number of years to become financially independent drastically. The beauty of turbo saving is that it's all about increasing your rate of saving and not worrying about whether your stock increased or decreased in value thus making it harder to target your freedom date. Turbo saving puts you in direct control of your plans not the stock market nor the economy. I planned how long it would take me to save $300,000 by investing $25,000 a year in salary. If I could save just $300,000 then I could quit my job and manage my investments going forward. It would take me 12 years ($300,000/$25,000) to be free. I did it in 10 years. Yes, you really can be free if you really want to.

OK IT'S TIME FOR YOU TO GET THE HANG OF THIS, CALCULATE YOUR OWN FINANCIAL FREEDOM DATE:

What I am trying to establish in your mind is the importance of having a plan. Having a definite number in mind that you feel that will give you financial freedom. I know it does not have to be exact. These are just a rule of thumb but you can make adjustments as you go along. So:

Multiply your normal annual expenses using the rule of 25; Example:

Step 1: $15,000 annual expenses x 25 = $375,000 amount of money to accumulate, your number.

Step 2: If you turbo saved 25% of your $70,000 income say $17,500 yearly in your 401k then how many years would you need to work to reach this amount? $375,000/$17,500 = 21.4 years, so in just 21.4 years you could be free. Keep in mind that the majority of working Americans has to work for 40 to 50 years just to retire with a measly social security check. Some Americans will never be able to retire after 40 – 50 years of work because they did not have a plan, and they have no savings. They simply spent all that they had. Here you are in control.

WORKSHEET

Things to remember	Actions To-Do	Dates

Step 3: Current Year: 2014, plus 21.4 years = Year 2035: financial freedom date. This is the year when you will become financially free. Keep in mind this is your roadmap. So you can adjust the saving rate whenever you choose. You can add more value and possibly get salary increases through the years. You can find other ways to increase your income, change jobs for better pay, start a business etc. If you were married and have two incomes then the years can be reduced by the increase in your saving rate. Let's say you save 50% of your income from your new job salary of $80,000. You will be able to cut the time to become financially free down drastically. This is what I did; I just kept increasing the amount I was willing to save until I got a time frame that I was comfortable with: 10 years instead of 40 years. You be the judge.

The beauty of turbo saving is that you are *not* relying on gains in the stock market to reach your freedom number. I mean, what if the stock market goes down just when you need your money forget that! Instead, you are relying on your increased savings (turbo saving), company matching funds and tax free compounding for your increases! Many people think that the bulk or their increase in their 401k plans will come from mutual funds gains. This is not true because of the uncertain volatility coupled with high, hidden fees that is stealing your gains you will never have enough to retire. However, when you turbo-save your money and rely on your cash build up in a simple 401k money market fund which is designed to preserve your principal, you can reach your goal a lot faster. Why, because with company matching and the ability to put more money to work plus you are not taxed on your money until withdrawals, this means that you will rapidly reach your goal. So with all of this extra money being added to my account I did not have to take on so much stock market risk in these stock mutual funds. I was weighted more to the "money fund" in my 401k. When you use a 401k with matching the company is paying you for the down market days and high hidden fees that are draining your account. And if you are in a high tax bracket like the middle class, then the government will give that money back to you in a tax refund. So there, *the IRS is paying you instead of you paying them*. Sure, you will pay tax either on the front end or the back end this is just one of the limited choices that we have to deal with. This is good for a change. Don't you agree? There is a section on investing in the later chapters.

<u>Ok now grab your calculator and make a plan and stick to it! What is your target freedom number</u>

WORKSHEET

Things to remember	Actions To-Do	Dates

ANNUITIES PAY INCOME

"There is a lack of financial education about the benefits of annuities and what's available"
- US Government Accountability Office

The main reason to consider an annuity is protection from loss and a guaranteed income that last a lifetime. If you live long enough often you will collect more in income than your initial investment.

An annuity is a contract between you and an insurance company that is designed to meet retirement and other long-range goals, under which you make a lump-sum payment or series of payments. In return, the insurer agrees to make periodic payments to you beginning immediately or at some future date.

Annuities can be great for providing income to meet your basic expenses so there is no need to place all of your "lump sum" into an annuity if you don't feel comfortable. Example: your basic expenses includes your home mortgage, utilities, food, insurance, taxes routine health care expenses etc. So, check around you see what's out there. Remember, you are not investing for a lump sum of money, you are investing for a reliable stream of income to meet your needs that you don't have to work for forever.

Annuities typically offer tax-deferred growth of earnings and may include a death benefit that will pay your beneficiary a specified minimum amount of money. While tax is deferred on earnings growth, when withdrawals are taken from the annuity, gains are taxed as ordinary income rates, and not capital gains rates. If you withdraw your money early from an annuity, you may pay substantial surrender charges to the insurance company, as well as tax penalties." Please go this SEC site and learn more about annuities so you can be well informed. www.investor.gov or call Investor Assistance (800) 732-0330.

There are a lot of confusions concerning annuities and it need not be. There are not a lot of open discussions about annuities because the investment community does not promote them. They are basically insurance contracts unlike a stock or mutual fund investment. Therefore, you won't see CNBC a channel dedicated to stock investments discussing insurance products. I believe every income earner should ultimately consider some type of annuity for retirement income. Why? Because an

WORKSHEET

Things to remember	Actions To-Do	Dates

annuity can provide income for life without working, a true money machine. As I said before I want you to change the way you think about investing and why you are investing. To me there is only one reason to invest your money, that is income, and annuities fit this description. However, before you consider an annuity, discuss the latest nuances with several reputable long-standing insurance providers.

TYPES OF ANNUITIES:

Deferred Annuities: These plans come with a wealth accumulation and a later payout phase. So, you get to choose when you want to start receiving income. With these plans, you do not pay any taxes on your wealth accumulation until you choose to start receiving income. Also at the same time, there can be a death benefit associated that you can leave to your heirs.

There are no limits to the amount of money that you can contribute to a deferred annuity. This is critical because traditional company sponsored pension plans 401k or Individual Retirement Plans place limits on the amounts that you can invest in these plans and receive a tax deduction and tax sheltered deferred growth. This can be a great bonus because you can make more contributions as you receive more money or maybe you have maxed out your other retirement plans but you want to contribute more to your retirement plans and still receive tax deferments. Education is key here so meet with your financial professional because annuities are also regulated by the states that you live in.

IMMEDIATE ANNUITIES:

These plans operate with a lump sum of money. They are great if you receive a lump sum from a bonus or a sale or maybe you hit the lottery and you want to convert this lump sum of money into a steady stream of income for life then an immediate annuity is great for that. These plans are designed to provide monthly income payouts immediately for you. Immediate annuities have a feature that will allow you to move a lump sum of money from your other retirement plans 401k, IRA into an immediate annuity plan. This will allow you to start receiving monthly income immediately. You can also move money from your deferred annuity to an immediate annuity and start receiving monthly income immediately as well

Annuities can be Variable, Fixed Rate, and Fixed Index i.e. tied to a stock market index:

Do you have a high-risk tolerance and want to take on more stock market risk? Then perhaps a variable annuity, which allows you to take advantage of market gains over the long term, is right for you. Do you want safety of principal at a fix rate of return? Then perhaps fixed rate annuities can provide you with a fix rate of return without the market fluctuations and safety of principle. On the other hand, perhaps you like the idea of participating in the stock market gains but not the losses then maybe a Fixed Index Annuity is best for you.

Again, make an appointment with your insurance provider so you can be educated on the pros and cons of these annuity plans before you purchase these contracts.

ADVANTAGES:

Guaranteed predictable source of income for life: Keep in mind that when you have a 401k retirement plan you are responsible for the results. When you purchase an annuity with a guaranteed income stream the provider is responsible for the results not you. A benefit to converting all or even a portion of your 401k or IRA retirement plan into an annuity plan, is that an annuity can provide you with income for the rest of your life and possibly your heirs as well. Also, when you transfer your taxed deferred retirement account to an annuity, the accumulations continue to grow tax deferred. However, the 10% penalty plus ordinary income tax still exist if you make a withdrawal before age 59 ½.

Flexible: Do you need more financial security then use the monthly payments from the annuity to buy a life insurance to leave more money to your love ones and or purchase long-term care insurance for yourself. *One of the benefits with annuities is that you can be creative. However, if you leave your savings in a retirement account it is possible that you can run out of money in these accounts leaving you with an insufficient income stream to meet your basic expenses in your retirement years. By choosing to purchase an annuity you are guaranteed never to run out of money, a true money machine.*

This is a significant feature of these annuities that you don't have with your retirement accounts. These annuities can be flexible to make up the short falls or gaps between your social security income and your retirement accounts in meeting your expenses. Say if you need an extra $900 to pay additional expenses then you can work with your insurance professional to purchase an annuity that will provide you with this extra income. Since you will only be using a portion of your total retirement funds, the rest of your money can continue to grow tax deferred to meet your unexpected expenses.

Riders: Riders are amendments to these annuities or insurance contracts that expands or restricts certain policy benefits that are guaranteed by the provider. They can also exclude other conditions from coverage. Since these additional riders are typically not guaranteed at the state or federal level, you want to make sure that the annuity issuer has the ability to pay. Keep in mind that the more riders you have the more they can reduce the amount of income that you receive on a regular basis. **There are many riders but the two most popular ones that seem to be of most interest:** *Guaranteed Lifetime Withdrawal Benefit Riders for* an income stream that last a lifetime and *Guaranteed Minimum Withdrawal Benefit Rider for* an income stream for a specified period of time.

DISADVANTAGES:

Liquidity: The biggest disadvantage of annuities is that they are not liquid in comparisons to other investments such as: saving accounts, stock and bond mutual funds where you can cash out with very little ease.

Fees: While annuities sound like a great plan for financial freedom and retirement there are certain fees that can limit the returns that you receive, so please discuss all fees i.e. hidden fees with your financial professional before you purchase an annuity. This will allow you to know your true cost.

Commissions: Most annuities are sold by brokers or sales people that can charge you as much as 10% of your principal.

High annual fees: Investments into certain kinds of annuities can result in annual expense fees, management fees and various insurance riders' fees.

Surrender charges: If you pull your money out of these insurance contracts before the surrender charge period schedule or within your first few years of purchase then you can face a hefty surrender charge which can run between 7% up to 20% for your first year. This fee usually declines a percentage point a year until it gets to zero.

ANNUITIES PROVIDERS MAKE THEIR PROFITS BY PUTTING A LIMIT ON YOUR RETURNS. THIS IS HOW THEY CAN AFFORD TO GIVE YOU INCOME GUARANTEES:

Cap and Floor Rate: Many index annuities apply upper limits that you can earn on your contract. Say if the S&P index returned 12% this year but your cap is 4% or whatever the agreed upon contracts states, then the maximum amount of gains that will be credited to your account will be only 4% not the 12%. The floor generally refers to a minimum guaranteed amount credited to your account. Say if the index loses 5% in a certain year your loss would be zero. So you have the upside without the down side.

Participation rate: This goes hand and hand with the cap rate. It's a percentage of the underlying index that the insurance company credits to your account. Say for example if the Index went up 12% and your participation rate was 50% then your account would be credited 6% or (.50 x 12%). If this account also has a cap rate of 4% as stated above, then your return will be limited to 4% and not the 6%. So, make sure you discuss and understand how these rates work before you make your purchase.

Spread/margin/asset fees: These are fees that are subtracted from the gains of the underlying index similar to the participation rates. Say if the index rise 12% and your annuity have a spread of 4% then 8% of the index gain will be credited to your account.

Point to point: is basically used for index annuities which refers to a period of time when interest will be credited to an account based on some underlying equity index i.e., S&P 500.

Annual Reset: refers to the length of time in which gain and losses in the index is measured and credited to your account. If there were a 10% gain in the index, this is further reduced by your interest cap or participation rate. So if you have a cap rate of 7% then 7% will be credited to your account that year not the 10%. The annual reset starts over again for another year. This reset can be monthly or quarterly. So consult your insurance professional.

HOW SAFE IS YOUR ANNUITY? *INSURANCE ON YOUR INSURANCE*:

Since you will be trading your money with an annuity provider or insurance company for a guarantee income stream to pay your expenses, you should demand a guarantee that the insurance company will be there when you need the income. One way to do this is to only deal with financially strong stable companies that have been in business for a number of years. Insurance companies are rated by Standard and Poor's, Moody's etc. Rating agencies can inform you of the company financial strength and integrity. These rating firms have their own grading scales from the strongest to the weakest companies. Therefore, you should only do business with the strongest and oldest rated companies. Generally, Fidelity Investments or, Vanguard are excellent companies that can provide assistance in your selections. The ratings are posted on-line, so discuss this with your insurance professional before you decide to purchase these insurance contracts.

It is the responsibility of the state insurance regulators to monitor the financial solvency of all the insurance companies that are licensed to do business in their state. This means that in the event of financial insolvency by an insurance company, the state's guarantee fund job is to protect you the policyholders. One of the ways in which they do this is attempting to transfer your policy to an insurance company that is stable. In the event this does not work then the state will administer your annuity through its central guarantee fund. However, your contract will be subject to the coverage limitations set by each state. So, it's a good idea before you purchase an annuity to go online to your State Insurance Guaranty and determine your state guarantee limit.

PAYING TAXES ON YOUR ANNUITIES: If you purchase your annuity with money that is pretax from a retirement account such as an IRA or 401k then the entire balance would be subject to ordinary income tax when you make withdrawals. But, if you make the annuity purchase with after tax money then you are taxed ordinary income tax on the earning only. However, if you purchase an annuity within a Roth IRA then withdrawals are generally tax free as long as you meet other Roth/IRA, IRS holding requirements. Basically, age of 59 ½ and assets held for 5 years. When it comes to taxes on annuities, consult your tax professional where you will discuss a term call an "exclusion ratio". This ratio maybe applied to taxable annuity payment to determine which portion of the payment is excludable from gross income.

USING SOCIAL SECURITY AS A DEFERRED ANNUITY: By delaying your social security benefits it is the same as getting an extra 8% a year in your paycheck. To me this is the same thinking as buying a deferred annuity. Therefore, if you want extra protection against outliving your income and you are in good health of course, then maybe just postpone receiving your social security until perhaps age 70. You can still receive Medicare benefits without receiving social security. But, of course you must have other sources of income to pay the bills. However, by delay receiving your social security checks until age 70 this will allow you to receive an extra income inflation adjustment provided by the social security administration. It acts like a deferred annuity. So again, education is key. Make an appointment with your local social security administration office that services your area of just run the numbers at the social security website online.

SOCIAL SECURITY PAY INCOME

The Social Security Administration (SSA) was designed to force you to contribute small amounts of money over your working years so you can have a guaranteed income stream in your retirement years for life**. *The good news is that since you are living longer there are very high odds that you will receive more in benefits than you contributed into the system***. Social security benefits provide more than just monthly income, it provides disability insurance, survivor benefits for young children, and the surviving spouse caring for the children. Politicians often refer to the SSA as a government entitlement program. Entitlements because they believe that the projected payouts are more than the contributions. So, efforts need to be made to adjust or modify the program because the government can't continue to afford it. The SSA collects a combined 15.3% in taxes from you and your employer thru payroll deductions. But after collecting all this money they are discussing cutting or delaying benefits because the fund is running out of money. This is the main reason that you should not rely solely on the SSA but you should invest your money in things that pay you income for life. Below is the truth from the Social Security Administration:

Social Security is the major source of income for most of the elderly.

- Nine out of ten individuals age 65 and older receive Social Security benefits.
- Social Security benefits represent about 38% of the income of the elderly.
- Among elderly Social Security beneficiaries, 52% of married couples and 74% of unmarried persons receive 50% or more of their income from Social Security.
- Among elderly Social Security beneficiaries, 22% of married couples and about 47% of unmarried persons rely on Social Security for 90% or more of their income.

An estimated 165 million workers are covered under Social Security.

- 51% of the workforce has no private pension coverage.
- 34% of the workforce has no savings set aside specifically for retirement.

According to the libertarian Cato Institute: *Past and current generations will pay $71.3 trillion in payroll taxes but will receive $93.4 trillion in benefits*. Adjusting for past and future transfers from the federal Treasury, the difference between "paid-in" and "paid-out" works out to $21.6 trillion.

The data shows you that even though you are forced to pay this tax now, you will get a return on your money when you need it most, in your retirement years.

WHO PAYS FOR MY SOCIAL SECURITY?

Let's start out by saying that your social security benefits are income for life without working. A true cash cow machine. You cannot outlive your paychecks. They will keep coming forever! You and your employer will contribute a total of 15.3%, into your fund each year. 12.4%, to the Social Security Trust Fund and 2.9%, for Medicare insurance. Here's how it's broken down:

YOUR CONTRIBUTION: A tax of 6.2% is withdrawn from your paycheck each year to a cap of $118,500, for the tax year 2015. This amount can increase each year with inflation. However, only about 5 to 6% of all the workers will earn more than the cap $118,500. So just about, everybody will pay this amount on his or her entire income. Additionally, you will pay a Medicare insurance tax of 1.45% on all of your wages, no cap here.

YOUR EMPLOYER CONTRIBUTION: Employers will match and pay an additional tax of 6.2% and 1.45% for you as well for a combined employee and employer 15.3% contribution to your Social Security retirement fund.

SELF-EMPLOYMENT CONTRIBUTION: As a self-employed business owner, you will contribute the employee and employer share and pay a tax of 15.3% (12.4% and 2.9%). However, you will get a tax deduction for the employer's share of the taxes.

FACT: NOT EVERYONE QUALIFIES FOR SOCIAL SECURITY BENEFITS, DO YOU?

To Qualify for Social Security: You must qualify to receive benefits under the social security administration laws. A worker must pay into the social security system a minimum amount of taxes for at least 40 quarters or 10 years. The years need not be paid consecutively just as long as you get the years of payments in there if you were born 1929 and after. Once you have reached your required quarters then next you have to determine your Full Retirement Age (FRA) for maximum benefits. ***However, you can qualify to receive reduced benefits at earliest age of 62***. Also when you have met your qualifications under certain circumstances certain members of your family are eligible as well. Go to the www.socialsecurity.gov website for the latest updates and set up your account and track your benefits.

The age requirements to receive FRA :

- If you were born in the years 1943 to 1954 your FRA is 66 years old
- If you were born in the years 1955 to 1959 your FRA is 66 years old plus
- If you were born in the year 1960 going forward your FRA is 67

THE AGE THAT YOU DECIDE TO START RECEIVING BENEFITS CAN IMPACT YOUR BENEFIT PAYOUT:

1. **Reduced Benefits:** If you start to receive benefits at the earliest age of 62 then your benefits will be permanently reduced up to approximately 20 to 30%

2. **Full benefits.** If you begin receiving benefits at you FRA then you are entitled to your full amount with no reductions, but no increases as well.

3. **Increased benefits**. If you start receiving benefits between your FRA and age 70 then you are entitles to a permanent increase of up to 32%

HOW MUCH MONEY DO I GET?

Simply put the more that you earn over a 35 year inflation adjusted period the bigger your check will be up to a maximum imposed by the social security administration.

That maximum for 2014 for a single worker who retired at FRA or 66 years old is $2,642. If you choose to begin collecting benefits at 62 then your check will be reduced up to approximately 30% of your FRA amount, this permanent reduction that cannot be undone under normal circumstances. Keep in mind that COLA or the "Cost Of Living Adjustments" are paid on the reduced amount as well. However, to keep you from collecting early and straining the crippling system you can get the maximum payout the social security provide a bonus system for you. If you decide to postpone collecting benefits starting at your FRA then they will pay you an additional 8% a year until you reach the age of 70. This could mean a maximum payout of 32% higher or around a monthly paycheck of $3,500 in 2015. Check with the social security website for updates.

They will pay you an extra 8% per year starting after you reach your FRA that 66 for 2015, in which they will give you an extra 8% per year starting at your FRA that is 66, in 2015. You are eligible to receive this bonus if you wait until you are 70 years old to start collecting.

While it is true that most people claim benefits before reaching the FRA due to many reasons mostly financial need or health reasons. You know if you retire before Medicare kicks in at 65 then you will still have to pay for your own insurance and that could be costly. Many seniors cannot find jobs so that is another factor that weights in on your personal decision to take retirement benefits as early as 62 years old. Many seniors I spoke with while doing this research collect benefits early because of job loss and working part-time at Walmart just does not cut it.

There are excellent benefit calculators at the www.socialsecurity.gov website. You can even open an account to track your benefits. I recommend this strongly. This will alert you to problems in your account sooner rather than waiting later. So go over and check it out.

because certain suspension rules may apply. The rules can change so make sure you get all the facts from the Social Security Administration before you claim benefits.

Whether you claim as soon as you are eligible or wait until later the numbers will work out just about the same. Social security payouts are based on your life expectancy. At full retirement age between 66 and 67 depending on your birth, you are eligible to receive 100% of your benefits. If you further wait until you are 70 to start collecting, you are rewarded with approximately 32% more in benefits than you would have received if you start collecting at full retirement age. The truth is that if you start collecting early than your full retirement age, you will receive smaller checks over a longer period. Conversely, if you wait until you are older you will

SHOULD I TAKE MY MONEY SOONER OR LATER?

This is an excellent question one that requires you to develop a plan in advance with all the facts before you began to claim your benefits. Your goals for personal freedom, health and financial condition should be major considerations in your decision-making. If you start to receive your benefits only to decide against it, seek the Social Security Administration for help
receive larger checks over a shorter period. Retirees will have to understand that receiving benefits are a needs based question but you can do as I did below. Go to the Social Security Administration website, and input your personal information and you will get results that will help you make your decisions.

This calculation below comes from the www.socialsecurity.gov benefits calculator website. I provided the random information below:

Below are estimated benefit amounts for retirement at 3 different ages, including your normal (or full) retirement age (67). We assume you will work every year up to the year in which you begin receiving benefits.

As shown in the table, you can receive a monthly benefit starting at age 62 and 1 month that would be reduced for life due to early retirement. If you choose to delay the start of benefits to a higher age, you can then receive a larger monthly benefit for the rest of your life.

For example, if you start taking benefits at age 62 and 1 month, you will receive $1,149 per month for the rest of your life. However, if you wait until age 67 to start receiving benefits, you will get $1,722 for the rest of your life. Therefore, by waiting until age 67, you can then receive $573 more per month than if you started lower monthly benefits at 62 and 1 month. Remember, these estimated figures are in today's dollars.

Social Security benefits are the foundation on which to build a financially secure retirement. Savings and pensions also are key components of your retirement plan."

Information you submitted
Date of birth: **6/15/1962**
Current earnings: **$55,000.00**
Benefit in **year-2015** dollars

Retirement Benefit Estimates

Retirement age	Monthly benefit amount
62	$1,149.00
67	$1,722.00
70	$2,195.00

Above we just concentrate on getting the biggest payout. At first, it appears that waiting 8 full years from age 62 when you are first eligible to receive benefits with monthly benefits of $1,149 and age 70 the monthly benefit practically doubles to $2,195.

Let's make our decision based on a breakeven analysis: The time between the ages of 62 and 70 is eight year or 96 months. So you will give up receiving 96 months of $1,149 = $110,304 just to wait until you are 70. The question is what will you do with the money? Consume it or invest it for greater returns? This is personal. I just hope I made the above decision making a little easier for you. Again, you should just look at social security benefits as another income stream to make you more wealthy. That is to create income to live on without working forever. As I see it whether you chose to retire early or wait until later I believe that you will receive the same amount of benefits over time.

EXAMPLE OF AN "AGE BREAK EVEN ANALYSIS"

I feel that you still have questions. Ok look at it another way using a break even age analysis or when all things being equal the age you will have to be for the two starts dates 62 and 70 start benefits dates to be the same.

Example: Say, Bill decided to receive his benefits as soon as he becomes eligible at age 62. For the sake of ease, let's use nice round numbers. So assume he will receive $750 monthly. It Bill would have waited until his full retirement age at 66 he would receive $1,000 monthly a full 25% increase. Now, if Bill would have started receiving his benefits at age 62 as oppose of waiting to receive benefits at full retirement age of 66 he would have already collected a total of $750 x 12 months x 4 years = $36,000.

If Bill had waited until age 66 at full retirement age to start receiving benefits he would collect an additional $250.00 a month or $1,000 monthly. The **question** is simply how long would it take that extra ($750 - $1,000) $250 per month to equal the $36,000 that Bill has already collected during those 4 years? **Answer:** A full 12 years ($36,000/$250 extra = 144 months or 12 years). Bill would have to wait a full 12 years or age 78 to receive the same benefits if he started at age 66. Saying it another way if Bill lives to be 78 (66 + 12 = 78) he would have effectively broke even on his decision to start receiving benefits at age 66, rather than starting to collect early at age 62.

Invest Your Social Security Paychecks For Greater Returns

Keep in mind that our calculations and benefits of receiving your paychecks early have a side benefit that we did not discuss, and that is investments. If the math works out for you then talk to your financial professional about other guaranteed investments where you can earn a return on your social security payouts.

Example: Say, at age 62 you start receiving after tax social security paychecks of $1,000 a month. If you don't need to spend these checks and can invest for a compound 5% return, then you can have approximately $116,067 by age 70, or $339,995 at age 80 and on and on. Here we are not considering taxes on your benefits.

If You Work While Collecting Your Benefits, Your Money Maybe Reduced!

If you want to keep all of your social security payouts then listen up. To keep 100% of your benefits you will have to know in advance the impact of working while you claim benefits. ***If you are at or over the full retirement age then there is no limit to the amount of money that you can earn, your benefits will not be reduced. If you are below full retirement age and you decide to continue to work and become a Barista at your local Starbucks or a Greeter at Walmart either full or part time your benefits can be reduced if you earn over a certain dollar.***

In 2015, if you were under your full retirement age you can earn up to $15,480 before your benefits are reduced. For every $2 over that limit, $1 will be withheld from your benefits. The year that you reach full retirement age for every $3 over your maximum of $41,400, the social security administration will withhold $1 from your benefits. These reductions are not lost forever they will be added to your benefits once you reach full retirement age. It is all about knowing your options before you file to collect benefits. So keep watching the yearly updates at www.socialsecurity.gov.

PAYING TAXES ON YOUR SOCIAL SECURITY INCOME

TIP: If you don't want to be taxed on your social security income, then develop a plan now before it's too late. Talk to your tax professional on how you can stay below your taxable threshold when you retire.

Unbelievably but after working 40 years or more and paying Social Security taxes, you may have to pay federal taxes if your combined income is over a certain dollar amount. Always discuss with your tax professional to determine what is considered earned income under the social security administration definition. Let's get started:

Individual Filers: For 2016, if you have combined taxable income that is reported on your tax returns as an individual and your combined income is between $25,000 and $34,000 you may have to pay income taxes on up to 50% of your social security benefits. If your combined income is over $34,000, up to 85% of your benefits may be taxable.

Married Joint Filers: For 2016, if you and your spouse have a combined income between $32,000 and $44,000 you will be taxed on up to 50% of your benefits. And if you earn more than $44,000 you will be taxed on up to 85% of your benefits. *Ok, the good news: no one will be taxed on more than 85% of their benefits. There I hope this helps.*

A SMALL BUSINESS PAY INCOME

There are only 3 ways to profit from a business; 1) Earn Income 2) distributions and dividends 3) Sale of the business.

The question to ask yourself is that how do you plan to profit from this business? What is the purpose of this business? Remember we are talking about financial security and freedom. You are financially free when you don't have to work for money anymore. You do what you love to do and you don't need to worry about money. To me this is freedom the American dream, income for life without working. With this goal in mind, let's proceed in determining how we can create or invest in a business with the goal of receiving an income for life without working.

Without much thought, most of us create and invest our money into a small business only with the purpose of earning money. To me the problem of working to earn money is just that, you must work to earn money, and when you stop, the money stops. You see the problem here? I think you should set up your small business so that one day you will be able to receive income from the business without working. So with this in mind you need to setup your business with a bigger vision than just making money. As a small business mentor and consultant, I would always advise small business owners that they should focus on the change that the business is trying to make. Focusing on the change that you want to make will give you and your business a laser like focus or a mission. This is what is needed to succeed, not starting a business just to make money. Starting a business just to make money is a true recipe for failure. As you know 90% of all businesses are out of business within the first five years. There is a different way to look at this.

Most people start a business because they do not want anybody to tell them what to do. However, they find themselves working 100 hours a week and never earning enough to expand the business because they need the paycheck that the business is providing. So, they are never able to create enough money to reinvest and grow the business. This is why you see small businesses staying small for generations and never growing. The goal should be to earn enough from the business so they can stop working and let others run the business and they sit back and earn dividends or distributions as the company make profits. This is income without working which should be your goal.

Business structure Sole proprietor vs. S-corporation: Changing your business from a mom and pop or sole proprietor to an S-Corporation will allow you to keep more of what you earn. You will be able to reduce your taxes because not all your income will be taxed for the FICA called the self-employment taxes or payroll taxes. For the year 2016, any self-employed person with income up to $118,500 will pay a FICA **tax** of 15.3% (12.4% for Social Security **tax** plus 2.9% for Medicare **tax**) on the business net income. As I personally found out, this is a big hit to your business bottom line and growth potential. Buy changing your small business to an S-Corporation, you can receive your cut of the business profits as dividend income.

You will receive a portion of the profits based on your shares of stock ownership in the business.

If you are considered an independent contractor and is operating your business as a sole proprietor with an income over $35,000, then it makes economic sense that you consider the benefits, legal protection, and tax saving of converting your business to a S-corporation. So it's best to start your business as an LLC then as the business become profitable you can elect to be treated as a S-corporation for tax purposes. Your CPA can assist you with this.

Keep in mind that when you elect as S-Corp, you are viewed by the IRS as the business owner and the employee. This is good because you can pay yourself a reasonable salary and pay yourself dividends which shields a portion of your income from self-employment taxes. This can be a huge savings. You keep more of what you earn! Another side benefit of an S-Corp is that if the business does not work out then you can possibly qualify for unemployment benefits unlike an LLC or sole proprietor where you are not considered an employee

Tax Savings Example

In the scenario below see the tax saving difference between operating your business as a sole proprietor vs. an S-Corp. Assume that Bob's Better Beer Company earns $80,000 in net income. As a sole proprietor, Bob would pay 15.3% or $12,240 for self-employment taxes. However, if Bob was an S-Corp, per the IRS, he paid himself a reasonable competitive salary of $40,000 the self-employment tax would be only $6,120. The remaining $40,000 would be paid to Bob as a dividend and not subject to the 15.3%, self-employment taxes for a total saving of $6,120. As you can see, an S Corporation generated significant savings more than $6,000 per year. This example does not include federal income taxes. The question that I ask a business owner is: why would you pay more taxes when you don't have to? This is how you keep more of what you earn.

WORKSHEET

Things to remember	Actions To-Do	Dates

Sole Proprietor		S-Corporation
Net Income	$80,000	$80,000
		divided by: Salary = $40,000 Dividends = $40,000
Net Income X Self-Employment Tax = $80,000 x 15.3% =		Salary X Self-Employment Tax = $40,000 X 15.3% =
Tax due $12,240		$6,120
Tax Saving		**$6,120**

When we talk about the only reason to earn and invest money is freedom. This means that you are free to do whatever you want and the income will flow from the business whether you are working or not. This is passive income or dividend income. So you are really looking to incorporate your business into a S-Corp and take a salary and dividend which will lower your taxes. Next you may want to leave the business owning a portion of the business through stock ownership. Then when cash dividends are declared or the company makes a cash distribution you will receive your check for life without working. Ultimately you want to be able to be a part owner in several businesses by purchasing shares of stock and receiving cash dividends or distributions for your share of the profits. You can either reinvest these profits in the business to grow the business or take your share of profits as cash dividends and go to the beach and just wait for the next dividend or profit sharing check to be automatically deposited to your bank account.

So, as you buy a business or start your own business or purchase stock in an existing business, you must understand your reason for how you plan to profit from the business. If freedom is your goal, then probably you want to invest in a business by owning stock. Then, if the board of Directors pay dividends you will receive your portion of the profits either monthly or quarterly deposited right into your bank account.

Example: You are a part owner of a medical practice as an equity investor and you paid $100,000 for 10,000 shares of stock in the company. If the medical practice earns a profit and the Board of Directors decides to pay a cash dividend of $5.00 per share annually. Then you can expect to receive $50,000 annually when the Board pays you your profits in dividends. This is income without working. True financial freedom.

Set Up Your Small Business To Pay You Income

The small business whether it's formed as a sole proprietor, S Corp, or LLC, it all should be for one single purpose in mind and that is financial freedom and security. Meaning that business owners must understand that they must grow their businesses so that they will be able to stop working at some point and just draw income or create a pension from the business. This is my biggest concerns with the health care professions. They make great incomes from their practices but they are horrible at creating passive income from their businesses. So, they work until they literally drop dead. My simple analogy to business owners is that if you are chief, cook and bottle washer and you do it all, well what happens when you must stop working? For most of these businesses the money stops. If your family is depended on your income, then if something happens to you their money will stop and their standard of living drops. So, the main lesson to learn as you read this section, is that you must organize your business so you can stop working and the money continue to flow. This is financial security the real American dream.

But there is hope for us, you see even though the tax law has more than 4 million words only 27 of these words tells us how to pay less on taxes and here it is: *26 U.S. Code § 162 - Trade or business expenses.*

"There shall be allowed as a deduction all the ordinary and necessary expenses paid or incurred during the taxable year in carrying on any trade or business"

Now this to me is the American Dream. There it is, just 27 words out of 4 million, which tells us the secret to wealth creation. Start a business for profit and tax benefits. Even if you fail in your pursuit to happiness, you can still reduce your taxes. **This is why I believe everyone should operate a small business in his or her spare time. That way while you are learning to be great at your business you can offset your taxes with your losses. In other words you can get a tax reduction with your losses while you are trying to build your business.** So make sure you conduct your business as a business and not a hobby. However, you can turn your hobby into a profitable business and receive all of the benefits of owning a legitimate business. Make sure you keep detail records of your profits and expenses for tax purposes. Out of all of the three, asset classes the riches people in the world became rich by starting a business, creating massive value and the money flowed to them as a result: Bill Gates- Microsoft, Steve Jobs – Apple, Warren Buffet – Berkshire Hathaway, Mark Zuckerberg – Facebook and other businesses. These men created their business and used the tax code to help them keep their profits by taking legal tax deductions that shield some of their income. So as you start your business remember those 27 words again.

One of the benefits of running your small business is that if you have losses you can use these losses to reduce your income from your job thereby reducing your taxable income.

Example:	Before	After
Your Salary	$80,000	$80,000
Small business loss	$0	($12,000)
Taxable income (AGI)	$80,000	$68,000

The tax law allows you to: *"There shall be allowed as a deduction all the ordinary and necessary expenses paid or incurred during the taxable year in carrying on any trade or business"*

So what are these words trying to tell us? That the tax law is written for the business owner the entrepreneurs not the wage slave. The tax law is written for those of who create jobs and provide services so the government doesn't have to. If you understand this then you know that taxes are an asset for those who understand them and a liability to those who do not. Fair enough? Make sure you get a copy of the IRS Tax Guide for Small Business Publication 334.

THE ADVANTAGES OF A SMALL BUSINESS:

Independence: Being in charge and being your own boss to me this is the biggest benefit because all of your creativity can be used to make you money not some big company who just view you as an expense and the last four digits of your social security number.

Freedom to create: As the owner of a business comes personal satisfaction, because you will be doing exactly what you love. Isn't that the real reason you went into business in the first place? You have talents and skills and now you can be as creative as you want to be.

Create Wealth: The possibility to become rich. This is how the rich got rich. Instead of being an employee, you get the full benefit of your own creativity and hard work.

Remember Bill Gates, Steve Jobs, Warren Buffet? These are just a few of the richest men on the planet, all started a small business.

Tax benefits: Big deductions. The tax benefits are too numerous to count but they can be used to help you run your successful business and keep more of the money that you earn. These tax benefits are just not available to the wage earner who earns approximately 50% on the dollar from an employer. However, if the wage earner starts a small business then they are instantly eligible for these big tax savings. Remember "There shall be allowed as a deduction all the ordinary and necessary expenses paid or incurred during the taxable year in carrying on any trade or business".

Example: Section 179 is a tax code created to help businesses. By allowing businesses to deduct the full amount of the purchase price of equipment (up to certain limits), Section 179 is a fantastic incentive for businesses to purchase, finance or lease equipment this year.

SMALL BUSINESS RETIREMENT PLANS ARE THE BIGGEST TAX SHELTERS

A self-employment retirement plans can reduce your tax bill now and can rack up tax-deferred investment gains for later. You can reduce your taxes from your business up to $53,000 for 2015, in a Solo 401k plan. Make sure you do not pass go on these plans. Grab a copy of the IRS Pub 560 Retirement Plans for Small Business. Also talk to your financial professional about the Simple IRAs and Solo 401k plans.

There are lots and lots of tax deductions allowed by the government for the small business entreprenuer. You can go to the IRS website for a copy of Publication 334, Tax Guide for Small Business. Also, consult with your CPA to ensure you take every legal deduction that you are allowed under the law.

DISADVANTAGES OF SMALL BUSINESS OWNERSHIP

Financial loss: The number one reason small business fail is a poor mismanagement of their money. Therefore, you should not co-mingle your business money with your personal bank accounts because you can cause more harm to your family security. Expenses in the beginning will be greater than profits and this equal loss. Depending upon what type of business you want to start there are different financial requirements and risk of loss as well. So beware of this and get as much financial knowledge as you did to create your product or service that you want to sell.

Time management: If you are a sole proprietor meaning it's just you then time off may be a problem for you especially when you are just getting started. Many Americans go into business for themselves only to realize that if you are the sole owner when you stop the money stops. So being aware of this will allow you to plan accordingly.

Record keeping: When I talk to most small businesses about the topic of record keeping, they immediately think that I referring to just financial records, but the real issue is filing. Record retention of clients and customers records can become a legal issue. I have the biggest problem with filing papers in my office. Therefore, the best way to fix this problem is to take a ½ day out of every week and file those documents in order that you will be able to retrieve them when you need them.

Taxes: As an employee, your employer is responsible to withhold your taxes from your paycheck and remit to the IRS timely. As a small business owner, you are responsible for calculating and remitting the correct amount of taxes to the IRS quarterly and annually. There can be penalties for being late and under reporting of income. So work with your tax professional until you get the hang of this.

RENTAL REAL ESTATE PAYS YOU INCOME

Build a real empire using the banks money; create income for life without working through rents!

There are seven big reasons why I think that rental real estate is the best small business

1. *OPM: Use the bank's money. The banks are falling over themselves to loan you money because real estate makes the best collateral.*

2. *Appreciation: Property goes up in value over time, either through inflation or your own sweat equity.*

3. *Depreciation: You can write off the cost of the property over time which can create a tax shelter for your income.*

4. ***Big tax deductions:*** *Real estate is just like any other business. All ordinary and necessary cost are tax deductible.*

5. ***Pays for itself:*** *(tenants) Someone else is paying the mortgage for you.*

6. ***Income:*** *Rental property provides passive income for life without working.*

7. ***Pride of ownership:*** *It's yours, you own something of value to pass as a legacy.*

This is a place where you can build your fortune and the rewards will definitely outweigh the risk. Why do I say that? It's because you have three very powerful and rich partners every time you purchase rental properties? Do you want to know who they are? 1) Time value or inflation, 2) the government thru tax sheltered income and 3) OPM or the banks money.

Example: I bought a townhome for $77,000, and I used only $3,000 of my own money! Can you believe it? I controlled a property for just $3,000 the rest of the money came from the bank, OPM (others people's money). Later I moved and rented this property. My returns on this property now are infinite because thru rents I received all of my money back on my down payment of $3,000. Now, because of *TIME* the property is valued about $100,000 and I do not have to share the profits with the banks that took the risk on loaning me the money. I can borrow the equity from the house and keep all of the money.

My other partner is Uncle Sam. The government actually pays and subsidizes all homeowners with hefty tax deductions. Have you ever heard of the mortgage banks bail out? Yes, you have. My partner the government will actually bail out the mortgage banks that loans me the money. Therefore, they literally guaranteed your success as a real estate investor. Every heard of Donald Trump, now the President? Yes, you have. This guy has built a real estate empire using the banks money and is still a billionaire after declaring bankruptcy, I forgot how many times! Why, because over time real estate property values always go up and bail him out.

If you want to become a real estate investor you must: 1) first take a course or read books to understand the ups and downs of the real estate business. 2) have a steady stream of income. 3) make sure that you reduce your money sucking bad debt before you start investing. 4) finally, review your FICO credit scores because the banks will use this score to determine whether you will get access to their money. These steps will allow you easy access to the bank's money and will guarantee your success. Remember you make money in real estate when you buy. So, buy low and don't sell, rent it, and receive passive income for life without working.

Passive Income: Real Estate Rentals creates Passive Income. This is where I specialize in generating a steady stream of income month after month. I simply buy rental homes for cash flow. Passive income equals financial freedom. Remember the definition of financial freedom: *income for life without working*. Well this is the area you may want to consider. Passive income is a result of certain types of business transactions that you do not operate full time like rental property or certain types of investment partnerships.

So, passive income attracts the personality type of the specialist. Conrad Hilton was a specialist, he created the Hilton Hotels that specialized in hotel real estate only, this is where he has made his fortune. However, the biggest benefit to passive income is that you make the investment one time and the income continues for life so you become financially independent as you receive income for life without working. In addition, the biggest benefit is that it's taxed the least by the government. This is true for my real estate investments. Also, it's easy to get bank financing because the asset is the collateral for the bank so it's perfect for obtaining financial independence. I funded my entire investments here with borrowed money. I used very little of my money never more than 20% and the bank took the risk while I collect the income month after month year after year. This is the easiest path to retirement and financial freedom that I know of. Why don't more people do this I have no idea. But it requires that you specialize in this income because there is a lot of things that can go wrong. So, this not a speculators sport, you have to specialize in this area to stay on top of all the federal and state housing laws.

As discussed in the Tax section of this course, passive losses can only be offset by passive income. However, if you actively participated in the operation of the property and your AGI (adjusted gross income) is under $100,000, you can deduct up to $25,000 of passive losses against other income and thus reduce your total tax bill. For now, the $25,000 deduction starts to phase out between $100,000 and $150,000. However, losses can be carried forward to future years when income can offset losses or until you dispose of the property. As long as a taxpayer actively participates in management decisions i.e. new tenant approval, lease terms, scheduling repairs and capital expenditures, etc. for rental properties. He has met the criteria of actively participation in the real estate leasing activity. In addition, the taxpayer must have at least a 10% interest in the rental activity.

THE ADVANTAGES INVESTING IN REAL ESTATE RENTALS:

Everybody is a customer: Everybody needs and wants a place to live. We all grew up hearing that home ownership is the American dream and this remains a goal for most Americans whether they choose to buy or not. The government and the banks stands ready to assist us with guaranteed loans and minimal qualifications.

Physical asset: Hey, I can see it. I can drive buy it, I can touch it and I can take pride in painting it whatever color I choose. I can turn it into rental property and let the tenants pay the mortgage while I get all of the tax deductions associated with ownership.

Use debt the banks money: The banks will go into partnership with you. They will loan you most of the money to buy the property. This is a great advantage over any other business because all you need is a little money to control this moneymaking asset. These low down payments allows you to leverage your money and create a real estate empire. It is a great way to create income from rents for life without working!

Hefty tax deductions: Mortgage interest, house depreciation, maintenance, repairs, vehicle mileage, travel expense, home office deduction, employees, contractors and insurance expense deductions etc., just to name a few. There are so many tax deductions I can fill a page. So make sure you are getting all of your tax deductions. You should work with a CPA on this.

Tax-free cash flow: You can receive tax-free income from your rental properties. Why? Because the depreciation and mortgage interest deduction alone should be more than enough to offset your rental income possibly making your income tax free. In addition, if you decide to sell the property you will be taxed at a lower tax rate called long term capital gains taxation.

Take a write off against income from your job: Depending upon whether or not you are classified as an Active Investor or Real Estate Professional and your income level of course, you can qualify to reduce your taxable income from your job by up to $25,000. Imagine that! So if you are not familiar with these tax sheltered benefits discuss this with your CPA.

THE DISADVANTAGES INVESTING IN REAL ESTATE RENTALS:

Tenants: Your success as a real estate investor is largely dependent on the screening of the tenants that you select for your rental property. Choose the wrong tenants and you can have a few problems on your hands such as costly repairs. A well written lease agreement can protect you against a tenant that will not pay rent. To keep an eye on tenants, you must get out and visibly inspect or hire an inspector to inspect your property at least annually. However, this can be overcome by hiring a Property Manager, but you still must view your property yourself. So, it's a hands-on business not like investing in paper assets such as stocks or bonds.

Maintenance and repairs: From time to time you will incur these costs for the upkeep of the property. That's why it's very important to properly screen tenants. Most tenants will not take ownership of the property that they rent thus the cost of upkeep will fall on you. Sometimes the wrong tenant can cause damages that you will be liable for and this can eat into your profits.

Vacancy: High vacancy rates can cost you money. An asset is only an asset if it is producing income. Like Rich Dad says: if the assets takes money out of your pocket it's a liability. So make sure you budget for the times when your property is vacant. Vacancies will cost you money because you will have to pay for the mortgage, taxes, insurance, certain utilities, repairs, and maintenance cost.

Depreciation recapture: When you sell your rental property, the IRS will attempt to recapture all of the depreciation that you deducted over the years while owning the property. The recapture depreciation is taxed at 25%. However, it only applies to the gain on sale of the property.

HOW TO USE THE BANK'S MONEY

CREATE INCOME WITH THE BANKS MONEY

*"Give me a lever long enough and a fulcrum on which
to place it, and I shall move the world."*
– Archimedes

Do YOU WANT to create a real estate empire or grow your business but don't have the cash, then try a little leverage? Use the banks money as leverage to create wealth. This is the big secret of the mega rich. Warren Buffet, Bill Gates, Jeff Bezos founder of Amazon, Larry Page and Sergey Brin, founder of Google and every real estate investor on the planet to include myself all used credit and debt, OPM as leverage to grow their businesses and personal wealth exponentially. Even if we fail, hey, it's not our money, we just scrap the project and start over on another project all with OPM. It's not your money! Learn to use the bank's money. Give them a piece of the action, and let them share in the risk.

In fact, I believe that starting from scratch and creating wealth, it becomes absolutely necessary that you learn how to use debt as leverage. Simply put, the use of borrowed money or OPM as leverage is the ability to control a of lot assets with just a little of your seed money. Debt as leverage allows you to have the ability to utilize more than just your limited resources. When you learn the power of leverage, you can adopt and take advantages of opportunities and economic changes quickly. Leverage in this way can be viewed as speed, meaning the more leverage or debt that you have working for you the faster will be your journey to financial freedom.

So, dismiss the notion that all debt is bad for you because that would be the wrong thing to do no matter who is spewing this *"get out of debt"* nonsense. The fact is, in order to create wealth as fast as you can, one of the keys is to use debt as leverage.

I like leverage because it's like borrowing someone else cows and selling the milk. However, if someone steals the cows then I owe the cows. So always consider the downside of leverage. It can be great when things are good but it will work 100% against you when things go bad.

USE THE BANK'S MONEY TO MAGNIFY YOUR WEALTH CREATION FASTER:

Example: Tom wanted to get into the rental real estate business to create wealth for his family. His target home prices in the area that he lived were $100,000. Tom was only able to save $10,000 a year from his job. His options were to:

A) Save $10,000 and after that one year get a bank loan as a form of leverage for the remaining 90% of the balance that he needed.

B) Work for 10 years saving $10,000 a year until he can afford to make the purchase of the rental home only to find out that the home is now priced at $110,000 due to appreciation.

Tom chose option A. He realized by using debt as leverage he can buy faster than had he waited for 10 years and still would not have saved enough money to buy the rental home. Leverage is key to financial freedom.

HOW YOUR HOME CAN PAY YOU INCOME

If you are a homeowner, then you are well on your way to creating lasting wealth. Depending on how long you have been a homeowner you are probably sitting on a goal mind beneath your feet and don't even know it. Let me explain.

I believe that your home is one of the biggest assets that you will own. I say asset because it will appreciate over time and this is an asset as far as I am concerned. You should be able to borrow the appreciated equity from your home and invest it in assets that create more money for you. This is good constructive debt. You are turning your home purchase or bad debt into good debt. How do you do this? You get home equity mortgage and you purchase a rental property or some other asset that will go up in value and pay you income for life. However, you should never use your home equity to buy depreciating asset like cars, consumables, jewelry etc. The asset that you purchase must pay the loan back and provide you a return or income stream.

When you pay the loan back, the government subsidizes you. **Example:** Say your federal tax rate is 25%. If you take out a mortgage at 5% this means that 25% of your

5% mortgage interest rate is tax deductible. This means that your real rate that you pay is only 3.75% not 5%. I bet you are really starting to like the taxman aren't you?

TWO COMMON TYPES OF HOME EQUITY LOANS

Home Equity Line Of Credit (HELOC):. A HELOC works just like a credit card. The bank establishes a line of credit for you based upon your qualifications and you can use it for a down payment on rental real estate that produces enough cash to make the payments plus a profit for yourself, or as seed money to invest in a profitable business. *Since this is borrowed money you must not use it to purchase consumer goods*. Financial freedom is all about making your money work for you not you working for money. In addition, the interest on the HELOC is tax deductible so it lowers your taxes as well. So why wait years to save up the $10,000 down payment for a rental home when you probably have the equity sitting right there trapped in your home.

Second mortgage: A second mortgage is a loan in addition to your first mortgage. Your bank will assist you in qualifying for a second mortgage. To qualify for this type of loan all you need is equity in your home or put it another way your home must have increased in value since you bought it. To qualify the bank will order an appraisal to see how much equity that you have in your home. Say, if your home is valued at $200,000 and you owe $100,000 you have $100,000 in home equity. The bank based on your qualifications usually will allow borrowing up to 80% of this equity. Another benefit is that the interest paid on certain of these second mortgages are tax-deductible based on the IRS guidelines.

Need to invest in your child education you can take either a second mortgage or a home equity line of credit (HELOC). Either a second mortgage or a HELOC will give you access to fund your child's college education or provide you capital to make other investments and the interest is all tax deductible.

DON'T SEND EXTRA MORTGAGE PAYMENTS TO THE BANK

I can think of three reasons why you should not send extra money to the bank to pay off your mortgage. 1) Sending extra money to the bank will decrease your monthly cash flow that you need to create wealth through investments. **2)** It makes it harder to save enough money to create an emergency fund for unexpected events such as a job loss. **3)** You can use these extra payments to create wealth by investing in a tax deferred retirement plan such as a 401k and receive extra money company matching.

Keep in mind that mortgage interest is simple interest, meaning that you only pay interest on the remaining balance. Also, the IRS helps you by giving you tax deductions for interest payments. It's the volume or total amount of interest that you pay over the life of your mortgage that's a concern for most people. Now if you want to earn compound interest then just invest these extra payments into a 401k, you will get compound interest meaning you earn interest on top of interest plus you get a tax deduction for investing your money. So, your money grows exponentially and this will make you wealthy.

How I Use Those Extra Mortgage Payments To Create Wealth And Income

I never make extra payments to pay off my personal mortgage because I use the growing equity to fund my other rental real estate deals that pay me more income. Also, these rentals create huge tax deductions as well. Listen, your home will still appreciate at the same rate if you pay more principal or not. A friend of mine at my last job was making extra payments to pay off his home early. He had no other savings because he was focusing all of his money on making extra payments on his mortgage. Then the economy took a down turn and he was laid off due to cutbacks.

He thought that because he made all of those extra advanced payments that the banks would let him skip a couple of payments if he wanted to. Well he was wrong. By paying extra payments, he created more equity by paying down his loan balance. Obviously, the banks foreclosed on his family and took the house because they can sell it at a lower price for a quick sale to pay off the remaining loan balance. The lesson: making extra payments is better for the banks because they have little risk remaining if you decide to default on the loan. However if making extra payments make you feel good then go ahead. I knew people that raced to pay off their mortgages only to turn around and take out a second mortgage. *Then why give the bank your money only to borrow it back and pay them more interest? Go figure!* There are Reverse mortgages being sold to older Americans. They provide loans based on the equity or value of your home. However, with a Reverse mortgage, you borrow money and you don't have to pay it back but they get to keep your home when you die or move out not your heirs. Maybe there is a better way? Ok consider this:

WORKSHEET

Things to remember	Actions To-Do	Dates

Example: One of my homes was valued at $154,000 when I bought it. This is a rental home now that appreciates approximately 5% yearly. In 4 years of me owning the property it was valued at $170,000. Money and wealth created out of thin air. I made no extra payments at all. I used this extra $16,000 and invested it in my other rental homes and created more income. Now this house would have been worth $170,000 if I had made extra payments or not. It does not matter the house will still appreciate over time. Most people use this extra equity buildup to buy cars, vacations and other things that depreciate in value. Therefore, they become poorer. Investing the extra equity in things that goes up in value and that pays you extra income so you can pay off the loan and keep the profits is what makes you wealthy and financially free!

So my plan was just to max out my 401k and other investments accounts and receive more tax deductions which allowed me to save even more. Within 10 years, my investments grew enough in all of my investments accounts that I could have paid off my mortgage in cash if I wanted to. Why? Because in my 401k account, I was getting company matching, stock appreciation, dividend gains, compound interest, my contributions were tax deductible and all of this money was being accumulated and growing all tax-free until I make withdrawals for income. So can you see why I chose not to make extra payments? Instead of taking 30 years to pay off the same house, I was able to do it in 10 years if I wanted to and I had a lot of money left over. The normal fixed mortgage interest is simple interest applied to the outstanding balance daily. It's not compound interest, which pays interest on top of interest. I was being paid compound interest and I was getting a tax deduction on my investments. Clear enough?

Example: Purchase price $154,000, appreciation $170,000 Wealth created $16,000

My rental appreciation during the year was:	$170,000 x 5% = 8,500
My $95,000 in my retirement investment accounts:	$95,000 x 8% = 7,600
Total Gains	$32,100
Taxes that I owe:	$0
If I take my $95,000 pay down my mortgage my profits that year only:	
	$170,000 x 5% = $8,500

Notice that there is no difference in the value of the home. The appreciated value of the home is $170,000. If I had used the $95,000 to pay down my mortgage balance, it would be

USE DEBT AS LEVERAGE IN YOUR BUSINESS

Two local bakeries regularly compete for the same customers every day. Because of this they both earn about the same income because they are located just two blocks from each other. The first bakery named; The Coffee Shop and the second bakery named; The Donut Shop earned about $15,000 in profits monthly. They both wanted to purchase a $120,000 automated assembly line to speed up the donut making process and double their profits.

The Coffee Shop decided that it did not want to go into debt to make the purchase but decided that it would save $10,000 a month and buy the equipment in one year with cash no debt.

The Donut Shop decided to leverage its current profits and decided to take a loan now. The business used its current earning to qualify for the loan and planned to pay the bank back from the increase profits. This is called leveraging the bakery profits.

Next Year:
The Coffee Shop saved the $120,000, to make the purchase but the price of the equipment is now $140,000 so they had to go back and save more money.

The Donut Shop last year decided to borrow the money needed to purchase the assembly line machine and since then they have been earning instead of $15,000 monthly, he has doubled his profits to $30,000 monthly using this new assembly line. Less the cost of borrowing at $3,000 monthly so net profits is $27,000 a month. You see by using debt as leverage The Donut shop has doubled its profits and the Coffee shop is still waiting. Debt as leverage makes you wealthier faster.

USE DEBT AS LEVERAGE INVESTING IN STOCKS

The only reason to borrow money to invest in high quality dividend paying stocks is that you can build wealth as the stock price increases and pays dividend income over the long term. We are not talking about using investment loans for making short term trading buying and selling stocks because the risk is just too great. Using these investments loan as leverage is something I would recommend for the skilled long-term investor. The skill sets required here is to choose stocks that will go up over time and pay dividend income. This way you will be creating wealth and an income stream faster than if you had just used your limited resources. You are using the banks money or a Brokerage Margin Account- OPM as leverage to create wealth and the loan simply magnifies your returns.

Example: Tom a skilled stock investor invested $10,000 of his own money to buy XYZ stock at $20 a share. The stock paid $2.00 a share dividend at year-end. The stock gained 10% at year-end. Tom profits looks like this:

Stock	10,000/$20 = 500 shares
Stock gain year one 10%	($20 x 10% =$2.00) so 500 shares x $2
	gain = $1,000
500 shares x $2 stock dividends	$1,000
TOTAL RETURN	$2,000

Tom can borrow $10,000 to leverage his profits from his stock brokerage margin account but decided to borrow against his home equity:

Stock	$20,000/$20 = 1,000 shares
Stock gain year one 10%	($20 x 10% =$2.00) so 1,000 shares x $2 gain = $2,000
Stock dividends $2 per share 1000 shares x $2.00 dividend =	$2,000
RETURN	$4,000
Loan interest at 5% less his 25% tax deduction = 3.75% x $10,000 =	($375)
TOTAL RETURN	$3,625

By using OPM as leverage Tom almost doubled his profits! All using the banks money! Lesson, learn to use debt to increase your profits. Of course, he could have lost 10% instead of gain but the dividends still bailed him out. You see having a long-term horizon and investing in quality stocks that pay a hefty dividend, you will win in the long term. I would not advise new investors to use debt as leverage starting out but once you become skilled this is what is possible and this is the rich man's secret: "debt".

You should always talk to your financial advisor before you invest in stocks because these people have the detail information that you need and the research to support your investment ideas. Investing in stocks can be risky.

Creating Wealth: is all about your savings rate and using debt as leverage. The three benefits for using debt as leverage:

1.   Give you the power to make the purchase quicker,

2.   You can repeat the purchases at a faster pace,

3.   Put you in control of the assets.

I used these three factors in my rental real estate business. I was able to control a lot of property for only a fraction of the purchase price. Leverage is a necessary ingredient to financial freedom.

GOOD CREDIT GIVES YOU THE KEYS TO THE BANKS MONEY

The famous criminal Willie Sutton was once asked why he robbed banks? His response was simple, eloquent, and humorous:
Because that's where the money is.

Where do you go when you need a loan? To the bank, Why? Because that's where the money is. Instead of robbery, you can use your good name to walk right out the front door of the bank with their money not yours and best yet no cops will be chasing you. Listen, the banks do not make any money unless they make loans so they are always looking for good opportunities to loan you money. That's why they shove it out the door to you in credit cards and home mortgages. They need to make loans to make money or they will go out of business. What you need is the keys to the banks money. The keys to the banks money is your good name and a great FICO score. That's it! From here, your wealth creation is guaranteed, just as mine was, guaranteed! Listen folks, all of you already have credit cards. In other words, the bank has trusted you with their money, so if you borrow their money to make you more money, then just pay them back with a little interest. And if you pay it all back at the end of the month in many cases you don't need to pay them any interest. What a deal! In addition, the credit card loans are unsecured, so the bank takes the risk. So, maintaining a good FICO score is very important to your rapid wealth creation and that's what this section is all about.

Simply stated, if you need money, then go where the money is.

The goal is to have the highest credit rating possible that will allow you to qualify for the lowest interest rate possible.

Learn to use credit to make you money not take your money!

Good Credit Puts Money in Your Pocket

Good management of your credit can lead you to the highest credit scores possible. Good credit scores leads to lowest cost of borrowing.

The purpose of credit is to make your life easier by having access to money when you need it. To me there is only one good use of credit, and that is, to use other people's money (OPM), to invest in things that goes up in value and pays me income. In other words, assets that make you more money! It was never supposed to be used as an everyday spending shopping spree. Keep in mind that each time you use your credit card or take a loan that this is bad debt and you will have to pay it back with interest and in some cases, there can be a penalty on top of the interest as well if you are late. This is why the banks will take a chance on you in the first place because they make a killing on interest and penalties. Simply stated they get rich and you get poorer.

The problem is that people have been given access to credit without the knowledge of the proper use of this powerful tool. The result is misuse, bankruptcy, and paying higher rates for perishable items like food and groceries, etc. If you buy, perishables like food with your credit card you must pay it off at the end of the month, do not carry a balance because you will be paying 15% for what you are flushing down the toilet. The second worse thing to do with your credit is to buy depreciating assets like I Phones, Tablets, TVs, computers, cars etc. This is where most of us get into trouble because we still have the debt and interest payments but the assets is now worth less that what we originally paid for it and we are still making the payments. The best and Gold Standard is to borrow at a lower rate and lend it at a higher rate or buy appreciable assets that goes up in value and produces income for you so you won't ever have to work for money. Other than that, I really don't see any use for borrowing money.

Example: Jim a very creditable friend of Bob asked for a collateralized loan of $1,000. He agreed to repay Bob in one year plus he would give him $200.00 or 20% for the use of the money and the title to his $12,000 motorcycle as collateral for the loan. Bob did not have the $1,000 but his grandmother had a couple of thousands tucked safely under her mattress. Bob made a deal with his grandmother that if she loaned him $1,000 for one year, he would pay her back and give her an extra $100.00 or 10%. Well grandma know that 10% is better that no interest because that is what her money was earning under the mattress. So she wrote Bob a promissory note for $1,100 payable in 12 months. Bob takes the $1,000 and lends it to Jim. They drew up a promissory for $1,200 payable in 12 months. At the end of 12 months, Jim brings Bob $1,200 per the note. Bob takes the money to his grandmother and pays her $1,100 keeping $100 for himself.

What did Jim do for the money? Nothing, he made money out of thin air. His very own money machine. This is what I do in my rental real estate homes. I use the banks money to make a deal. I put very little of my money down and the bank takes the risk. I make money every month without any work. To me this is the proper use of credit and this is how you create wealth. This is where I want you to focus your attention on how to use OPM to create wealth in half the time.

DEVELOP A POWERFUL CREDIT PROFILE AND GAIN ACCESS TO THE BANK'S MONEY

One of the major keys to open the banks vault is your FICO (Fair Isaac Corporation) credit scores. An estimated 90% of all moneylenders use FICO scores in deciding whether they are going to lend you any money. This score is the most widely used by lenders, insurers, and job applicants just to name a few.

So, if you want to apply for a credit card, an apartment, home mortgages, and car loans, a line of credit, or buy life and health insurance, your FICO score will certainly be considered. A low score can prevent you from getting the loan to buy your dream home or that fancy apartment that you want or, worse yet, make you ineligible for some jobs. That's why it is very important to your wealth creation that you understand how your FICO score is calculated, what the score means, and how you can improve your score.

FICO scores generally ranges from about 300 to 850 and they are the standard credit score used in this country. Also, FICO scores are used in just about all of lending decisions. So the higher your FICO score the lower the interest rates that you will be charged to borrow money. I have talked to many bankers in my real estate deals so I am speaking out of experience here. My banker explained to me how my score was created: 1) 35% is based on my payments history, 2) 30% the total amount that I owe, 3) 15% the length of my credit history, 4) 10% any new credit and 5) 10% the types of credit I use, i.e. loan sharks are not a good type of credit.

To get a free copy of your report go to: www.annualcreditreport.com. See what they are saying about you and your credibility! They will explain to you how to review your report and correct any errors that is negatively affecting your ability to get the lowest possible interest rates.

Exam: Bob's 30-year mortgage:

Loan	FICO	Interest rate	Payment	Total interest
$220.000	**620**	8.275%	$1,890	$226,356
$220,000	**720**	3.75%	$1180	$110,453
		Saving:	$710	$115,903

As you can see just by having a higher FICO score you saved $710 a month in payments and over the life of the mortgage a saving of $115,903. Now are you convinced that you must manage your FICO score? This is just one example. When you include your credit cards, employments, car loans, insurance premiums the cost could be in the hundreds of thousands of dollars over your lifetime.

HOW TO IMPROVE YOUR CREDIT SCORE STARTING TODAY

So, what can you do to start creating the highest FICO score possible? Remember, that your score is considered in practically all of the loans that you will qualify for, so it's worth your attention. To accumulate wealth in the shortest time possible you will have to use borrowed money, this is what is called leverage. Below are some action steps that my bankers helped me to improve my score and qualify for lowest interest rates on my loans.

Payment History: Start today to pay your bills on time no more late fees.

Total Amount Owed: Review your credit cards balances and make sure that you only use less than a third of total available credit.

Length of Credit History: Lenders are looking for a track record so you may want to apply for some type of credit today and make regular payments just to establish a good payback record. So get started today, the sooner the better.

New Credit: Do not apply for unnecessary credit. I had a problem with this one. Every time I went into a big department store, they always offered me a discount if I can qualify for a new credit card. I had no idea that when I was turned down it counted against my score.

Types of Credit Used. Mortgage, car loan, and credit cards are typical types of credit. Stay away from loan sharks like E-Z Money Payday loans.

My bankers instructed me to strive for a FICO score above a 740. This is considered a good credit score and will save you thousands of dollars in interest payments.

Note: FICO scores calculations may change from time to time so make sure to keep up to date on all changes. This can have a significant effect on your score.

MY STRATEGY TO QUICKLY RAISE YOUR CREDIT SCORE

My strategy is to focus on the biggest areas that matters. Since "Payment History and Total amount owed" makes up 65% of my score then I make sure that I manage these two areas because they will have the biggest immediate effect on your credit score.

PAYMENT HISTORY:

MAKE SURE ALL ACCOUNTS ARE CURRENT!

The first thing you should do annually is to get a current copy of your credit report and make sure all accounts are current. You want to bring "current", all past due accounts even if you have to pay the minimum payments that is required by the due dates. It is most important to pay as agreed! So get caught up.

MAKE SURE ALL ACCOUNTS ARE YOURS AND CORRECT!

Since the two biggest areas are payment history and total amount owed, you want to make sure that all account listed are yours and are accurate. If you detect any errors, request a correction today. You may need to submit copies of your documents to dispute errors not originals to the credit bureaus. The credit bureaus are required to investigate within 30 days. Then they must get back to you within 45 days of the outcome of their investigation. This can increase and make an immediate huge impact on your score. I have had some accounts evaporated using this method. Keep in mind that current accounts are 35% of your total FICO score.

ARRANGE TO PAY OFF OLD ACCOUNT BALANCES IF POSSIBLE:

These old items can damage your FICO score and bad information can stay on your credit report for up to seven and ten years depending on the type of information. Try to call these old creditors and make some type of payment arrangement with them. Sometimes they will even reduce the amount owed and stop collection efforts. You can even add a written explanation to your credit report. Get any agreement in writing. You can do this yourself no need to hire credit counselors. Try not to borrow money with a low FICO score because if you get the loan you can bet that you will pay the highest interest rates to borrow that money. Therefore, this subject is worth your immediate attention.

TOTAL AMOUNT OWED:

REDUCE THE TOTAL AMOUNT THAT YOU OWE ON CREDIT AVAILABLE TO YOU:

The amount of debt that you carry vs. your allowable credit limit can work for you or against you. Your debt utilization rate is calculated based on the amount of debt that you owe compared to the amount of credit that is available to you. What you are aiming for is a debt utilization rate of 30% or lower. You can achieve this quickly by paying down credit card debt first and this will make a big impact on your FICO score.

OK, let's get to work, get a copy of your annual report and let's get some credit! Remember, good credit gives you access to other people's money.

In the following Appendices, I have provided additional blank copies of the tables that will assist you in completing this money course. Consider this money course as a guide for you as you move along to become wealthy. Now that you have a system in your hands that puts you in control of your financial destiny. You now have the means to live your life on your terms with the money to enjoy it.

You really can be free from a routine life of poverty. Remember, wealth is a choice, poverty is the result from not making that choice.

Until we meet again, keep what you earn, use your money to make you wealthy, not them!

Good luck!

APPENDIX SECTION

A

CASH FLOW WORKSHEET

INCOME	BEFORE	AFTER	CHANGE
My take home paycheck			
Spouse take home paycheck			
Government			
Pension/Retirement			
Investments			
Other			
TOTAL MONTHY INCOME			

EXPENSES

CATEGORY	EXPENSE	BEFORE	AFTER	CHANGE
ESSENTIALS	Food			
	Clothing			
	Medical			
	Education			
	Child/Pet Care			
	Other			
HOUSING	Mortgage/Rent			
	Utilities			
	Phones			
	Maintenance/Repair			
	Other			
TRANSPORTATION	Auto loan payments			
	Oil/Gas/parking/tolls etc			
	Other			
ENTERTAINMENT	Dining			
	Cable TV			
	Internet Service			
	Other			
INSURANCE	Life			
	Home			
	Auto			
	Medical			
	Other			
INVESTMENTS	Bank/Cash			
	401ks/IRAs			
	CDs			
	Brokerage			
DEBT	Credit Cards payments			
	Personal loans payments			
	Student loans payments			
	Other			
	TOTAL MONTHLY EXPENSES			
CASH FLOW STATEMENT		BEFORE	AFTER	CHANGE
TOTAL MONTHLY INCOME				
subtracted				
TOTAL MONTHLY EXPENSES				
equal TOTAL MONTHLY CASH FLOW				

A

CASH FLOW WORKSHEET

INCOME	BEFORE	AFTER	CHANGE
My take home paycheck			
Spouse take home paycheck			
Government			
Pension/Retirement			
Investments			
Other			
TOTAL MONTHY INCOME			

EXPENSES

CATEGORY	EXPENSE	BEFORE	AFTER	CHANGE
ESSENTIALS	Food			
	Clothing			
	Medical			
	Education			
	Child/Pet Care			
	Other			
HOUSING	Mortgage/Rent			
	Utilities			
	Phones			
	Maintenance/Repair			
	Other			
TRANSPORTATION	Auto loan payments			
	Oil/Gas/parking/tolls etc			
	Other			
ENTERTAINMENT	Dining			
	Cable TV			
	Internet Service			
	Other			
INSURANCE	Life			
	Home			
	Auto			
	Medical			
	Other			
INVESTMENTS	Bank/Cash			
	401ks/IRAs			
	CDs			
	Brokerage			
DEBT	Credit Cards payments			
	Personal loans payments			
	Student loans payments			
	Other			
	TOTAL MONTHLY EXPENSES			

CASH FLOW STATEMENT	BEFORE	AFTER	CHANGE
TOTAL MONTHLY INCOME			
subtracted			
TOTAL MONTHLY EXPENSES			
equal TOTAL MONTHLY CASH FLOW			

B

Table 1- Living Expenses/Monthly

Mortgage/ Rent payments

    (include taxes, insurance

      dues etc.) $_____

Groceries $_____

Utilities (phone, electric, water etc.) $_____

Insurance (health, life, auto) $_____

Medical (prescriptions, doctor visits) $_____

Transportation (gasoline, oil, taxi, buses, fees) $_____

Child Care (school, support etc.) $_____

Miscellaneous expenses $_____

    TOTAL $_____

B

Table 1- Living Expenses/Monthly

Mortgage/ Rent payments

    (include taxes, insurance

       dues etc.) $_____

Groceries $_____

Utilities (phone, electric, water etc.) $_____

Insurance (health, life, auto) $_____

Medical (prescriptions, doctor visits) $_____

Transportation (gasoline, oil, taxi, buses, fees) $_____

Child Care (school, support etc.) $_____

Miscellaneous expenses $

       TOTAL $_____

C

Table 2 - Liabilities (Installments Debts)

Name of Creditor	Minimum Monthly Payments
	$
	$
	$
	$
	$
	$
	$
	$
	$
	$
	$
	$
	$
	$
	$
TOTAL	$

C

Table 2 - Liabilities (Installments Debts)

Name of Creditor	Minimum Monthly Payments
	$
	$
	$
	$
	$
	$
	$
	$
	$
	$
	$
	$
	$
	$
	$
TOTAL	$

D

Table -3 Income

Sources of Income	Monthly
My take home Paycheck	$_____
Spouse take home Paycheck	$_____
Support /Alimony	$_____
Tips	$_____
Government (unemployment, etc)	$_____
Pension/Retirement	$_____
Part Time	$_____
Military	$_____
Commissions	$_____
Passive/Investments/Savings	$_____
Other (Welfare, family, etc)	$
TOTAL INCOME	$_____

D

Table -3 Income

Sources of Income	Monthly
My take home Paycheck	$_____
Spouse take home Paycheck	$_____
Support /Alimony	$_____
Tips	$_____
Government (unemployment, etc)	$_____
Pension/Retirement	$_____
Part Time	$_____
Military	$_____
Commissions	$_____
Passive/Investments/Savings	$_____
Other (Welfare, family, etc)	$_____
TOTAL INCOME	$_____

E

Table 4 - Summary Table

Finally let's compile these totals into one easy read table

Total "Living Expenses" from Table -1 $_____   A

Total "Installment Debt" from Table -2   + $_____   B

Total of Living Expense plus installment Debt $_____ A + B

Your Income from Table -3 $_____   C

Total Cash Flow
*"Subtract (A + B) from C for positive/negative cash
flow"* $_____

E

Table 4 - Summary Table

Finally let's compile these totals into one easy read table

Total "Living Expenses" from Table -1 $_____   A

Total "Installment Debt" from Table -2   + $_____   B

Total of Living Expense plus installment Debt $_____ A + B

Your Income from Table -3 $_____ C

Total Cash Flow
"Subtract (A + B) from C for positive/negative cash flow" $_____

F

Net Worth Statement Worksheet	
ASSETS	
Cash stored at home	$_____
Cash in Checking Acct	$_____
Cash in bank/credit union (emergency fund)	$_____
Saving Accounts (emergency fund)	$_____
Money Market Accounts	$_____
Market Value of Home	$_____
Estimated Value of Household Items (furniture, paintings, etc)	$_____
Market Value of Other Real Estate & Land	$_____
Stocks	$_____
Bonds	$_____
Mutual Funds	$_____
Market Value of Vehicles (www.nadaguides.com)	$_____
Cash Value Life Insurance (not term insurance)	$_____
Current Value of retirement plans(401K,403b etc)	$_____
Individual Retirement Account (IRA, Roth)	$_____
Estimated Value of Personal Items (jewerly, clothes, etc)	$_____
TOTAL ASSETS	$_____
LIABILITIES	
Home Mortgage	$_____
Home Equity Loan	$_____
Other Real Estate Loans (Rentals, Vacation etc)	$_____
Auto Loan or Lease	$_____
Credit Card Balances	$_____
Student Loans	$_____
Other Liabilities/Loans	$_____
TOTAL LIABILITIES	$_____
NET WORTH **(Total Assets minus Total Liabilities)**	$_____

F

Net Worth Statement Worksheet	
ASSETS	
Cash stored at home	$_____
Cash in Checking Acct	$_____
Cash in bank/credit union (emergency fund)	$_____
Saving Accounts (emergency fund)	$_____
Money Market Accounts	$_____
Market Value of Home	$_____
Estimated Value of Household Items (furniture, paintings, etc)	$_____
Market Value of Other Real Estate & Land	$_____
Stocks	$_____
Bonds	$_____
Mutual Funds	$_____
Market Value of Vehicles (www.nadaguides.com)	$_____
Cash Value Life Insurance (not term insurance)	$_____
Current Value of retirement plans(401K,403b etc)	$_____
Individual Retirement Account (IRA, Roth)	$_____
Estimated Value of Personal Items (jewerly, clothes, etc)	$_____
TOTAL ASSETS	$_____
LIABILITIES	
Home Mortgage	$_____
Home Equity Loan	$_____
Other Real Estate Loans (Rentals, Vacation etc)	$_____
Auto Loan or Lease	$_____
Credit Card Balances	$_____
Student Loans	$_____
Other Liabilities/Loans	$_____
TOTAL LIABILITIES	$_____
NET WORTH **(Total Assets minus Total Liabilities)**	$_____

G

EMERGENCY EXPENSES	Montly payment	How many months	Total Funds
Emergency savings account total			

G

EMERGENCY EXPENSES	Montly payment	How many months	Total Funds
Emergency savings account total			

H
MY DEBT MANAGEMENT TABLE

Creditor whom I owe	My Balance Due	Interest Rate	Minimum Monthly Payment	Minimum Payment plus Bonus	Pay off Sequence	Results of Debt Management Process	More money created from interest savings	FICO

H
MY DEBT MANAGEMENT TABLE

Creditor whom I owe	My Balance Due	Interest Rate	Minimum Monthly Payment	Minimum Payment plus Bonus	Pay off Sequence	Results of Debt Management Process	More money created from interest savings	FICO

WORKSHEET

Things to remember	Actions To-Do	Dates

WORKSHEET

Things to remember	Actions To-Do	Dates

www.ingramcontent.com/pod-product-compliance
Lightning Source LLC
Chambersburg PA
CBHW080803180526
45168CB00006B/2320